Reading to Learn Hebrew

the Progressive Torah

Level One

בְּרֵאשִׁית

Genesis

Black & White Edition

טhe Pרogרessive Toרaה is a production of
Minister 2 Others

Third Edition

English Scripture modified
from the 1917 Jewish Publication Society

ISBN 978-1-947751-07-1
Copyright © 2017 Minister 2 Others
Minister2others.com

*May you be blessed by this work,
and may you draw closer to יהוה
by reading
טhe Pרogרessive Toרaה*

Introduction

The Progressive Toרה was created as a means by which one may simply read the Torah and, as a byproduct of that reading, learn some Hebrew. This is what we call the *"Reading to Learn Hebrew"* method. It is a more natural way to study the language.

Genesis begins the Hebrew journey by restoring the name and titles of יהוה as well as all the direct quotes of יהוה the alef-tavs, and the conjugations of the various restored words. The focus of the restored words in Level One is the Creator and words that have to do with Him.

There are various colors used in this text:

    Hebrew names are indicated with a brown font: אַבְרָהָם (*Abraham*)
    Vocabulary words are indicated with a blue font: אֱלֹהִים (*Elohim*)
    (*these words will be dissected in the Index section*)
    Verbs are indicated with a red font: וַיֹּאמֶר (*And he said*)
    Words of יהוה are indicated with a green font: יוֹם (*Day*)
    Miscellaneous words are in black: עֶרֶב (*Evening*)

The formatting may be a little unconventional in some places to allow for the restored words of יהוה to be on the same page as the translation. This allows the reader to compare the restored Hebrew with the English translation because the translation is line for line.

For example:

	Line 1	יהוה	says...this
	Line 2	יהוה	says...that
	Line 3	יהוה	says...how

	Line 1	*Translation...this*
	Line 2	*Translation...that*
	Line 3	*Translation...how*

Also, the numbering of the verses can vary between English versions and Jewish versions so, where the numbering is not the same, both systems have been used. The English version in black, and the Jewish version in light blue. Here is an example of a dual numbered verse: (9) (32:10)

If the reader is not familiar with the Hebrew Alef-Bet, it may be prudent to get a copy of The Progressive Alef~Bet produced by Minister 2 Others, and learn the letters and vowels. This is not a necessary step in order to read through this series, it is only advised for those who would like the extra help.

Thank you for supporting the work at Minister 2 Others. May your journey through The Progressive Torah be exciting and insightful. May you see new things and experience great wonders. May you be provoked to seek יהוה as never before, that you may know His voice and be led by His hand!

Translations & Pronunciations

Along with restoring some of the Hebrew words, all the names of people and places have been transliterated.* Where this may have caused some confusion, the English translation of those words have also been included.

Pronunciation key:

Proper names are divided into syllables by a dash "-"

" a " as in the word awe
" ay " as in the word may
" e " as in the word bed
" <u>e</u> " as in the word they
" i " as in the word as in taxi
" ai " as in the word aisle
" o " as in the word go
" u " as in the word blue

" kh " is a rasping H sound like the ch in Bach

an apostrophe ' is pronounced like a schwa
(like the "e" in stupefy)

*To translate is to exchange meaning for meaning:
the Hebrew word אב means father.

To transliterate is to exchange sound for sound:
the Hebrew word אב is pronounced av.

Table of Contents

Chapter 1 1
Chapter 2 11
Chapter 3 15
Chapter 4 23
Chapter 5 28
Chapter 6 31
Chapter 7 39
Chapter 8 43
Chapter 9 48
Chapter 10 57
Chapter 11 60
Chapter 12 64
Chapter 13 68
Chapter 14 72
Chapter 15 75
Chapter 16 82
Chapter 17 86
Chapter 18 97
Chapter 19 106
Chapter 20 112
Chapter 21 116
Chapter 22 122
Chapter 23 128
Chapter 24 131
Chapter 25 142
Chapter 26 146
Chapter 27 153
Chapter 28 161
Chapter 29 166
Chapter 30 171
Chapter 31 179
Chapter 32 188
Chapter 33 195
Chapter 34 198
Chapter 35 202
Chapter 36 207
Chapter 37 211
Chapter 38 216
Chapter 39 221
Chapter 40 224
Chapter 41 228
Chapter 42 236
Chapter 43 242
Chapter 44 248
Chapter 45 254
Chapter 46 259
Chapter 47 264
Chapter 48 269
Chapter 49 274
Chapter 50 280
Index 284
Final Notes 302

Chapter 1

The Creation Day One

(1) בְּרֵאשִׁית (In the beginning) בָּרָא אֱלֹהִים (Elohim created) אֵת the sky וְאֵת (and *) the land.

(2) And the land was formless and empty, and darkness was over the face of the deep. וְרוּחַ אֱלֹהִים מְרַחֶפֶת (And the Spirit of Elohim was hovering) over the surface of the waters.

(3) וַיֹּאמֶר אֱלֹהִים (And Elohim said)

יְהִי אוֹר

Let there be light.

And there was light.

(4) וַיַּרְא אֱלֹהִים (And Elohim saw) אֵת the light כִּי-טוֹב (that it was good), and וַיַּבְדֵּל אֱלֹהִים (Elohim separated) between the light and the darkness.

(5) וַיִּקְרָא אֱלֹהִים (And Elohim called) the light

Day ~ יוֹם

and the darkness קָרָא (He called)

Night ~ לַיְלָה

וַיְהִי-עֶרֶב וַיְהִי-בֹקֶר (And there was evening and there was morning) the first day.

Genesis ~ 1

Day Two

(6) וַיֹּאמֶר אֱלֹהִים *(And Elohim said)*

יְהִי רָקִיעַ
בְּתוֹךְ הַמָּיִם
וִיהִי מַבְדִּיל
בֵּין מַיִם לָמָיִם

Let there be a vaulted dome
in the midst of the waters,
and let it be a separation
between waters to waters.

(7) וַיַּעַשׂ אֱלֹהִים *(And Elohim made)* אֵת the vaulted dome וַיַּבְדֵּל *(and He separated)* between the waters which were under the vaulted dome and the waters which were over the vaulted dome. וַיְהִי־כֵן *(And it was so).*

(8) וַיִּקְרָא אֱלֹהִים *(And Elohim called)* the vaulted dome

שָׁמַיִם ~ *Sky*

וַיְהִי־עֶרֶב וַיְהִי־בֹקֶר *(And there was evening and there was morning)* a second day.

Day Three

(9) וַיֹּאמֶר אֱלֹהִים *(And Elohim said)*

Level One   בְּרֵאשִׁית ~ א

יִקָּווּ הַמַּיִם

מִתַּחַת הַשָּׁמַיִם

אֶל־מָקוֹם אֶחָד

וְתֵרָאֶה הַיַּבָּשָׁה

Let the waters flow together

under the sky

to one place,

and let the dry [ground] be seen.

וַיְהִי־כֵן (*And it was so*)

(10) וַיִּקְרָא אֱלֹהִים (*And Elohim called*) the dry [ground]

Land ~ אֶרֶץ

and the collection of the waters קָרָא (*He called*)

Seas ~ יַמִּים

וַיַּרְא אֱלֹהִים כִּי־טוֹב (*And Elohim saw that it was good*).

(11) וַיֹּאמֶר אֱלֹהִים (*And Elohim said*)

תַּדְשֵׁא הָאָרֶץ דֶּשֶׁא

עֵשֶׂב מַזְרִיעַ זֶרַע

עֵץ פְּרִי

Let the land be vegetated with vegetation

herbage that will sow seed

fruit trees

Genesis ~ 1

עֹשֶׂה פְּרִי לְמִינוֹ
אֲשֶׁר זַרְעוֹ-בוֹ
עַל-הָאָרֶץ

making fruit for his species

which his seed is in him

on the land.

וַיְהִי-כֵן *(And it was so)*

(12) And the land brought forth vegetation, herbage sowing seed for his species, and a tree making fruit in which his seed is in him for his species. וַיַּרְא אֱלֹהִים כִּי-טוֹב *(And Elohim saw that it was good).*

(13) וַיְהִי-עֶרֶב וַיְהִי-בֹקֶר *(And there was evening and there was morning)* a third day.

Day Four

(14) וַיֹּאמֶר אֱלֹהִים *(And Elohim said)*

יְהִי מְאֹרֹת
בִּרְקִיעַ הַשָּׁמַיִם
לְהַבְדִּיל בֵּין הַיּוֹם
וּבֵין הַלָּיְלָה

Let there be lights

in the vaulted dome of the sky

to separate between day

and between night,

Level One בְּרֵאשִׁית ~ א

וְהָיוּ לְאֹתֹת
וּלְמוֹעֲדִים
וּלְיָמִים וְשָׁנִים

and let them be for signs
and for appointed times,
and for days and years,

(15)

וְהָיוּ לִמְאוֹרֹת
בִּרְקִיעַ הַשָּׁמַיִם
לְהָאִיר עַל־הָאָרֶץ

And they will be for lights
in the vaulted dome of the sky
to give light on the land.

וַיְהִי־כֵן *(And it was so)*

(16) וַיַּעַשׂ אֱלֹהִים *(And Elohim made)* אֵת two great lights אֵת the greater light to rule the day וְאֵת *(and *)* the lesser light to rule the night וְאֵת *(and *)* the stars.

(17) וַיִּתֵּן אֹתָם אֱלֹהִים *(And Elohim gave * them)* in the vaulted dome of the sky to give light on the land,

(18) and to rule over the day and over the night, and to separate light from darkness. וַיַּרְא אֱלֹהִים כִּי־טוֹב *(And Elohim saw that it was good)*.

(19) וַיְהִי־עֶרֶב וַיְהִי־בֹקֶר *(And there was evening and there was morning)* a fourth day.

Genesis ~ 1

Day Five

(20) וַיֹּאמֶר אֱלֹהִים *(And Elohim said)*

יִשְׁרְצוּ הַמַּיִם

שֶׁרֶץ נֶפֶשׁ חַיָּה

וְעוֹף יְעוֹפֵף עַל־הָאָרֶץ

עַל־פְּנֵי

רְקִיעַ הַשָּׁמָיִם

Let the waters swarm with

a swarm of living soul,

and a flyer shall fly over the land

across the faces of

the vaulted dome of the sky.

(21) וַיִּבְרָא אֱלֹהִים *(And Elohim created)* אֶת־הַתַּנִּינִם *(* the dragons)* the great ones וְאֵת *(and *)* every soul -- הַחַיָּה *(the living)*, the moving -- which the waters abound for their species וְאֵת *(and *)* every winged flyer for his species. וַיַּרְא אֱלֹהִים כִּי־טוֹב *(And Elohim saw that it was good)*.

(22) וַיְבָרֶךְ אֹתָם אֱלֹהִים *(And Elohim blessed * them)* לֵאמֹר *(saying)*

פְּרוּ וּרְבוּ

וּמִלְאוּ אֶת־הַמַּיִם בַּיַּמִּים

וְהָעוֹף יִרֶב בָּאָרֶץ

Be fruitful and increase,

and fill * the waters in the seas,

and the flyer shall increase in the land.

Level One   בְּרֵאשִׁית ~ א

(23) וַיְהִי-עֶרֶב וַיְהִי-בֹקֶר *(And there was evening and there was morning)* a fifth day.

Day Six

(24) וַיֹּאמֶר אֱלֹהִים *(And Elohim said)*

תּוֹצֵא הָאָרֶץ נֶפֶשׁ חַיָּה לְמִינָהּ

בְּהֵמָה וָרֶמֶשׂ

וְחַיְתוֹ-אֶרֶץ לְמִינָהּ

Let the land bring forth living soul for her species:

cattle and creeping thing,

and land animal for her species.

וַיְהִי-כֵן *(And it was so)*

(25) וַיַּעַשׂ אֱלֹהִים *(And Elohim made)* אֶת the land animal for her species וְאֶת *(and *)* the cattle for her species וְאֶת *(and *)* every creeping thing of the ground for her species. וַיַּרְא אֱלֹהִים כִּי-טוֹב *(And Elohim saw that it was good).*

(26) וַיֹּאמֶר אֱלֹהִים *(And Elohim said)*

נַעֲשֶׂה אָדָם

בְּצַלְמֵנוּ כִּדְמוּתֵנוּ

וְיִרְדּוּ בִדְגַת הַיָּם

We shall make man

in our image, like as us,

and they shall hold sway in the fish of the sea,

וּבְעוֹף הַשָּׁמַיִם
וּבַבְּהֵמָה וּבְכָל-הָאָרֶץ
וּבְכָל-הָרֶמֶשׂ הָרֹמֵשׂ
עַל-הָאָרֶץ

and in the flyer of the sky,
and in the cattle, and in all the land,
and in every creeping thing creeping
on the land.

(27) וַיִּבְרָא אֱלֹהִים *(And Elohim created)* אֶת the human בְּצַלְמוֹ *(in His image)* בְּצֶלֶם אֱלֹהִים *(in the likeness of Elohim)* בָּרָא אֹתוֹ *(He created * him)*, male and female בָּרָא אֹתָם *(He created * them)*.

(28) וַיְבָרֶךְ אֹתָם אֱלֹהִים *(And Elohim blessed * them)* וַיֹּאמֶר אֱלֹהִים *(and Elohim said)* to them,

פְּרוּ וּרְבוּ
וּמִלְאוּ אֶת-הָאָרֶץ
וְכִבְשֻׁהָ
וּרְדוּ בִּדְגַת הַיָּם

Be fruitful and increase,
*and fill * the land*
and subdue her,
and hold sway in the fish of the sea

Level One   בְּרֵאשִׁית ~ א

וּבְעוֹף הַשָּׁמַיִם

וּבְכָל־חַיָּה

הָרֹמֶשֶׂת עַל־הָאָרֶץ

and in the flyer of the sky,

and in every animal,

the one creeping on the land.

(29) וַיֹּאמֶר אֱלֹהִים (And Elohim said)

הִנֵּה נָתַתִּי לָכֶם

אֶת־כָּל־עֵשֶׂב זֹרֵעַ זֶרַע

אֲשֶׁר עַל־פְּנֵי כָל־הָאָרֶץ

Behold, I am giving to you

* every plant that sows seed

which is on the face of all the land,

וְאֶת־כָּל־הָעֵץ אֲשֶׁר־בּוֹ

פְרִי־עֵץ זֹרֵעַ זָרַע

לָכֶם יִהְיֶה לְאָכְלָה

and * every tree that in him

is the fruit of a tree sowing seed.

to you, it shall be for food.

(30)

וּלְכָל־חַיַּת הָאָרֶץ
וּלְכָל־עוֹף הַשָּׁמַיִם
וּלְכֹל רוֹמֵשׂ עַל־הָאָרֶץ
אֲשֶׁר־בּוֹ נֶפֶשׁ חַיָּה
אֶת־כָּל־יֶרֶק עֵשֶׂב לְאָכְלָה

And to every animal of the land
and to every flyer of the sky,
and to all creeping thing on the land
which in him is a living soul
* every green herbage for food.

וַיְהִי־כֵן *(And it was so)*

(31) וַיַּרְא אֱלֹהִים *(And Elohim saw)* אֶת everything that עָשָׂה *(He had made)* and, behold, it was טוֹב מְאֹד *(very good).* וַיְהִי־עֶרֶב וַיְהִי־בֹקֶר *(And there was evening and there was morning)* a sixth day.

Chapter 2

Sabbath Day

(1) And the sky and the land and all their host were finished.

(2) וַיְכַל אֱלֹהִים (And Elohim finished) בַּיּוֹם הַשְּׁבִיעִי (on the seventh day) מְלַאכְתּוֹ (from His work) that עָשָׂה (He had done) וַיִּשְׁבֹּת (and He rested) בַּיּוֹם הַשְּׁבִיעִי (on the seventh day) from all מְלַאכְתּוֹ (His work) that עָשָׂה (He had done).

(3) וַיְבָרֶךְ אֱלֹהִים (And Elohim blessed) אֶת־יוֹם הַשְּׁבִיעִי (* the seventh day) וַיְקַדֵּשׁ אֹתוֹ (and He sanctified * it) because on it שָׁבַת (He rested) from all מְלַאכְתּוֹ (His work) which בָּרָא אֱלֹהִים (Elohim created) לַעֲשׂוֹת (to do).

Garden Of Eden

(4) These are the generations of the sky and the land when they were created, in the day of עֲשׂוֹת יהוה אֱלֹהִים (YHVH Elohim making) land and the sky;

(5) before any plant of the field was on the land, and before any plant of the field had sprung up, because יהוה אֱלֹהִים (YHVH Elohim) had not caused rain upon the land, and there was no human being to cultivate אֵת the ground,

(6) but a mist would rise from the land and water אֵת the whole face of the ground.

(7) וַיִּיצֶר יהוה אֱלֹהִים (And YHVH Elohim formed) אֶת־הָאָדָם (* the human) of soil from הָאֲדָמָה (the ground) וַיִּפַּח (and He blew) into his nostrils נִשְׁמַת חַיִּים (the breath of life) and the human became a living creature.

(8) וַיִּטַּע יהוה אֱלֹהִים (And YHVH Elohim planted) a garden in E-den in the

Genesis ~ 2

east וַיָּשֶׂם *(and He put)* there אֵת the human whom יָצַר *(He had formed).*

(9) וַיַּצְמַח יהוה אֱלֹהִים *(And YHVH Elohim caused to sprout)* every tree that was pleasing to the sight וְטוֹב *(and good)* for food. And עֵץ הַחַיִּים *(the Tree of Life)* was in the midst of the garden וְעֵץ הַדַּעַת טוֹב וָרָע *(and the tree of the knowledge of good and evil).*

(10) Now a river flowed out from E-den that watered אֵת the garden, and from there it diverged and became four branches.

(11) The name of the first is Pi-shon. It went around אֵת all the land of the Kha-vi-lah, where there is gold.

(12) The gold of that land is טוֹב *(good)*; bdellium and onyx stones are there.

(13) And the name of the second is Gi-khon. It went around אֵת all the land of Cush.

(14) And the name of the third is Hi-de-kel. It flows east of A-shur. And the fourth river is P'rat.

(15) וַיִּקַּח יהוה אֱלֹהִים *(And YHVH Elohim took)* אֵת the human וַיַּנִּחֵהוּ *(and He left him)* in the Garden of E-den to cultivate it and to keep it.

(16) וַיְצַו יהוה אֱלֹהִים *(And YHVH Elohim instructed)* the man לֵאמֹר *(saying)*

מִכֹּל עֵץ־הַגָּן

אָכֹל תֹּאכֵל

From every tree of the garden

to eat, you shall eat.

(17)

וּמֵעֵץ הַדַּעַת

טוֹב וָרָע

לֹא תֹאכַל מִמֶּנּוּ

Level One

בְּרֵאשִׁית ~ ב

And from the tree of the knowledge of
good and evil
you shall not eat from it,

כִּי בְּיוֹם אֲכָלְךָ מִמֶּנּוּ
מוֹת תָּמוּת

because in a day that you eat from it
to die, you shall die.

Creation Of Woman

(18) וַיֹּאמֶר יהוה אֱלֹהִים *(YHVH Elohim said)*

לֹא-טוֹב
הֱיוֹת הָאָדָם לְבַדּוֹ
אֶעֱשֶׂה-לּוֹ עֵזֶר
כְּנֶגְדּוֹ

It is not good
being of the human for his aloneness.
I will make for him a helper
as his counterpart.

(19) וַיִּצֶר יהוה אֱלֹהִים *(And YHVH Elohim formed)* out of the ground every beast of the field וְאֵת *(and *)* every flyer of the sky וַיָּבֵא *(and He brought)* each to the human to see what he would call it. And whatever the human called that living creature was its name.

13

Genesis ~ 2

(20) And the human gave names to every animal and to the flyer of the sky and to every animal of the field. But for Adam there was not found a helper as his counterpart.

(21) וַיַּפֵּל יהוה אֱלֹהִים *(And YHVH Elohim caused to fall)* a deep sleep upon the human. And he slept וַיִּקַּח *(and He took)* one of his ribs וַיִּסְגֹּר *(and He closed up)* the flesh where it had been.

(22) וַיִּבֶן יהוה אֱלֹהִים *(And YHVH Elohim built)* אֶת the rib which לָקַח *(He took)* from the human for a woman וַיְבִאֶהָ *(and He brought her)* to the human.

(23) And the human said,

> "She is now bone from my bones and flesh from my flesh; she shall be called 'Woman,' for she was taken from man."

(24) Therefore, a man shall leave אֶת his father וְאֶת *(and *)* his mother and shall cling to his wife, and they shall be as one flesh.

(25) And the human and his wife, both of them, were naked, and they were not ashamed.

Chapter 3

Man Disobeys

(1) וְהַנָּחָשׁ (*And the serpent*) was crafty from every animal of the field which עָשָׂה יהוה אֱלֹהִים (*YHVH Elohim made*). And he said to the woman,

"Indeed אָמַר אֱלֹהִים (*Did Elohim say*),

'You shall not eat from any tree in the garden'?"

(2) The woman said to הַנָּחָשׁ (*the serpent*),

"From the fruit of the trees of the garden we may eat."

(3)

"But from the tree that is in the midst of the garden אָמַר אֱלֹהִים (*Elohim said*)

לֹא תֹאכְלוּ מִמֶּנּוּ

וְלֹא תִגְּעוּ בּוֹ

פֶּן־תְּמֻתוּן

You shall not eat from it,
and you shall not touch on it,
lest you die.

(4) And הַנָּחָשׁ (*the serpent*) said to the woman,

"You shall not surely die."

Genesis ~ 3

(5)

"For יָדַע אֱלֹהִים (Elohim knows) that on the day you eat from it, then your eyes will be opened and you will be כֵּאלֹהִים (like Elohim) knowing טוֹב וָרָע (good and evil)."

(6) When the woman saw that the tree was טוֹב (good) for food and that it was a delight to the eyes, and the tree was desirable to make one wise, then she took from its fruit and she ate. And she gave it also to her husband with her, and he ate.

(7) Then the eyes of both of them were opened, and they knew that they were naked. And they sewed together fig leaves and they made for themselves coverings.

(8) Then they heard אֶת-קוֹל יהוה אֱלֹהִים (* the voice of YHVH Elohim) walking in the garden לְרוּחַ (to the wind of) the day. And the human and his wife hid themselves from the presence of יהוה אֱלֹהִים (YHVH Elohim) among the trees of the garden.

(9) וַיִּקְרָא יהוה אֱלֹהִים (And YHVH Elohim called) to the human וַיֹּאמֶר (and He said) to him,

אַיֶּכָּה

"Where are you?"

(10) And he replied,

"I heard אֶת-קֹלְךָ (* Your voice) in the garden, and I was afraid because I am naked, so I hid myself."

(11) וַיֹּאמֶר (And He said)

מִי הִגִּיד לְךָ
כִּי עֵירֹם אָתָּה

Level One

בְּרֵאשִׁית ~ ג

Who told to you

that you were naked?

הֲמִן־הָעֵץ אֲשֶׁר צִוִּיתִיךָ

לְבִלְתִּי אֲכָל־מִמֶּנּוּ אָכָלְתָּ

From the tree which I instructed you

so as not to eat of - from it you ate?

(12) And the human replied,

> "The woman whom נָתַתָּה (You gave) to be with me -- she gave to me from the tree and I ate."

(13) וַיֹּאמֶר יהוה אֱלֹהִים (And YHVH Elohim said) to the woman,

מַה־זֹּאת עָשִׂית

What is this you have done?

And the woman said,

> הַנָּחָשׁ (The serpent) deceived me, and I ate."

Elohim Curses The Serpent

(14) וַיֹּאמֶר יהוה אֱלֹהִים אֶל־הַנָּחָשׁ (And YHVH Elohim said to the serpent)

כִּי עָשִׂיתָ זֹּאת

אָרוּר אַתָּה מִכָּל־הַבְּהֵמָה

Because you have done this,

you will be cursed from all the cattle

וּמִכֹּל חַיַּת הַשָּׂדֶה

עַל־גְּחֹנְךָ תֵלֵךְ

וְעָפָר תֹּאכַל כָּל־יְמֵי חַיֶּיךָ

and from every animal of the field.
On your torso you shall go
and soil you shall eat all the days of your life.

(15)

וְאֵיבָה אָשִׁית

בֵּינְךָ וּבֵין הָאִשָּׁה

וּבֵין זַרְעֲךָ וּבֵין זַרְעָהּ

הוּא יְשׁוּפְךָ רֹאשׁ

וְאַתָּה תְּשׁוּפֶנּוּ עָקֵב

And I will put hostility
between you and between the woman,
and between your seed and her seed;
he will bruise you on the head,
and you will bruise him on the heel.

Reproving the Woman

(16) To the woman אָמַר *(He said)*

הַרְבָּה אַרְבֶּה עִצְּבוֹנֵךְ וְהֵרֹנֵךְ

Level One   בְּרֵאשִׁית ~ ג

I will greatly increase your labor in pregnancy;

בְּעֶצֶב תֵּלְדִי בָנִים
וְאֶל־אִישֵׁךְ תְּשׁוּקָתֵךְ
וְהוּא יִמְשָׁל־בָּךְ

in labor you shall bear children.
And to your man shall be your desire
and he shall have dominion over you.

Reproving the Man

(17) And to A-dam אָמַר *(He said)*

כִּי־שָׁמַעְתָּ
לְקוֹל אִשְׁתֶּךָ
וַתֹּאכַל מִן־הָעֵץ
אֲשֶׁר צִוִּיתִיךָ לֵאמֹר
לֹא תֹאכַל מִמֶּנּוּ

Because you listened
to the voice of your wife
and you ate from the tree
which I commanded you saying
Do not eat from it

Genesis ~ 3

אֲרוּרָה הָאֲדָמָה
בַּעֲבוּרֶךָ
בְּעִצָּבוֹן תֹּאכְלֶנָּה
כֹּל יְמֵי חַיֶּיךָ

*The ground shall be cursed
on your account;
in labor you shall eat it
all the days of your life.*

(18)

וְקוֹץ וְדַרְדַּר
תַּצְמִיחַ לָךְ
וְאָכַלְתָּ אֶת־עֵשֶׂב הַשָּׂדֶה

*And thorns and thistles
shall sprout for you,
and you shall eat
* the herbage of the field.*

(19)

בְּזֵעַת אַפֶּיךָ
תֹּאכַל לֶחֶם
עַד שׁוּבְךָ אֶל־הָאֲדָמָה
כִּי מִמֶּנָּה לֻקָּחְתָּ
כִּי־עָפָר אַתָּה
וְאֶל־עָפָר תָּשׁוּב

Level One   בְּרֵאשִׁית ~ ג

In the sweat of your nose
you shall eat bread,
until your return to the ground
that you were taken from;
because soil you are,
and to soil you shall return.

(20) And the human named his wife חַוָּה (*Kha-vah /Eve*), because she was the mother of כָּל-חָי (*all life*).

Man Sent from the Garden

(21) וַיַּעַשׂ יהוה אֱלֹהִים (*And YHVH Elohim made*) for A-dam and for his wife garments of skin וַיַּלְבִּשֵׁם (*and He clothed them*).

(22) וַיֹּאמֶר יהוה אֱלֹהִים (*And YHVH Elohim said*)

הֵן הָאָדָם הָיָה

כְּאַחַד מִמֶּנּוּ

לָדַעַת טוֹב וָרָע

וְעַתָּה פֶּן-יִשְׁלַח יָדוֹ

וְלָקַח גַּם

Behold -- the human has become
like one from us,
to know good and evil.
And now lest he stretch his hand
and take also

מֵעֵץ הַחַיִּים
וְאָכַל וָחַי לְעֹלָם

from the Tree of Life
and he eats and he lives forever.

(23) וַיְשַׁלְּחֵהוּ יהוה אֱלֹהִים *(And YHVH Elohim sent him)* from the Garden of E-den, to till אֵת the ground from which he was taken.

(24) וַיְגָרֶשׁ *(And He drove out)* אֵת the human וַיַּשְׁכֵּן *(and He caused to tabernacle)* אֵת-הַכְּרֻבִים *(* the k'ru-vim/cherubim)* from the east of the Garden of E-den וְאֵת לַהַט הַחֶרֶב *(and * the flame of the sword)* turning itself to guard אֵת the way to עֵץ הַחַיִּים *(the Tree of Life)*.

Chapter 4

Cain And Abel

(1) Now the human knew אֶת Kha-vah *(Eve)* his wife, and she conceived and bore אֶת־קַיִן (* *Cain*). And she said,

קָנִיתִי *(I have acquired)* a man of אֶת יהוה (* *YHVH*)."

(2) Then she bore אֶת his brother Ha-vel (* *Abel*). And Ha-vel *(Abel)* became רֹעֵה *(a shepherd of)* sheep, and Ka-yin became a tiller of the ground.

(3) And in the course of time Ka-yin brought an offering from the fruit of the ground לַיהוה *(to YHVH)*.

(4) and Ha-vel *(Abel)* also brought an offering from the choicest firstlings of his flock. And יהוה *(YHVH)* looked with favor to Ha-vel *(Abel)* and to his offering,

(5) but to Ka-yin and to his offering He did not look with favor. And Ka-yin became very angry, and his face fell.

(6) And וַיֹּאמֶר יהוה *(YHVH said)* to Ka-yin,

לָמָּה חָרָה לָךְ
וְלָמָּה נָפְלוּ פָנֶיךָ
הֲלוֹא אִם־תֵּיטִיב שְׂאֵת
וְאִם לֹא תֵיטִיב

Why is it hot for you,
and why is your face fallen?
Is there not, if you do well, acceptance?
And if you do not do well,

לַפֶּתַח חַטָּאת רֹבֵץ

וְאֵלֶיךָ תְּשׁוּקָתוֹ

וְאַתָּה תִּמְשָׁל־בּוֹ

sin is reclining at the portal

and its desire is for you,

* *and you must take dominion over it.*

Cain Kills Abel

(8) Then Ka-yin said to his brother Ha-vel (*Abel*),

"*Let us go out into the field.*"

And when they were in the field, Ka-yin rose up against his brother Ha-vel (*Abel*) and killed him.

(9) וַיֹּאמֶר יהוה (*And YHVH said*) to Ka-yin,

אֵי הֶבֶל אָחִיךָ

Where is Ha-vel (Abel) your brother?

And he said,

"*I do not know; am I my brother's keeper?*"

(10) וַיֹּאמֶר (*And He said*)

מֶה עָשִׂיתָ

קוֹל דְּמֵי אָחִיךָ

צֹעֲקִים אֵלַי מִן־הָאֲדָמָה

Level One בְּרֵאשִׁית ~ ד

What have you done?
The voice of the blood of your brother
is crying to Me from the ground.

(11)

וְעַתָּה אָרוּר אָתָּה מִן-הָאֲדָמָה

אֲשֶׁר פָּצְתָה אֶת-פִּיהָ לָקַחַת

אֶת-דְּמֵי אָחִיךָ מִיָּדֶךָ

So now you are cursed from the ground,
*which has opened * its mouth to take*
** the blood of your brother from your hand.*

(12)

כִּי תַעֲבֹד אֶת-הָאֲדָמָה

לֹא-תֹסֵף תֵּת-כֹּחָהּ לָךְ

נָע וָנָד

תִּהְיֶה בָאָרֶץ

*Because you serve * the ground,*
it shall not continue to give its strength to you.
A wanderer and a fugitive,
you shall be in the land.

(13) And Ka-yin said to יהוה (*YHVH*),

"*My punishment is greater than I can bear.*"

(14)

"*Look, You have driven* אֹתִי *(* me) out today from the face of the* *ground, and from Your face I must hide. I will be a wanderer and a fugitive on the land, and it will happen that whoever finds me will kill me."*

(15) וַיֹּאמֶר יהוה (*And YHVH said*) to him

לָכֵן כָּל־הֹרֵג קַיִן
שִׁבְעָתַיִם יֻקָּם

*Therefore, any one who kills Ka-yin,
he will be avenged sevenfold.*

וַיָּשֶׂם יהוה (*And YHVH put*) אוֹת (*a sign*) for Ka-yin so that whoever found him would not kill אֹתוֹ (*him).

(16) And Ka-yin went out from the presence יהוה (*YHVH*) and he settled in the land of Nod, east of E-den.

Descendants of Cain

(17) And Ka-yin knew אֶת his wife, and she conceived and gave birth to אֶת Kha-nokh (Enoch). And when he built a city he named the city after his son Kha-nokh (Enoch).

(18) And to Kha-nokh (Enoch) was born אֶת I-rad, and I-rad fathered אֶת M'khu-ya-el, and M'khu-ya-el fathered אֶת M'tu-sha-el, and M'tu-sha-el fathered אֶת La-mekh.

(19) And La-mech took to himself two wives. The name of the first was A-dah, and the name of the second was Tzi-lah.

(20) And A-dah gave birth to אֶת Ya-val; he was the father of those who live in

Level One   בְּרֵאשִׁית ~ ד

tents and those who have livestock.

(21) And the name of his brother was Yu-val; he was the father of all who play stringed instruments and wind instruments.

(22) Then Tzi-lah also gave birth to אֶת Tuv-al~Ka-yin who forged all kinds of tools of bronze and iron. And the sister of Tuv-al~Ka-yin was Na-a-mah.

(23) Then La-mekh said to his wives,

> *"A-dah and Tzi-lah, listen to my voice; wives of La-mekh, hear my words. I have killed a man for wounding me, even a young man for injuring me."*

(24)

> *"If Ka-yin is avenged sevenfold, then La-mekh will be avenged seventy and seven."*

Birth of Seth

(25) Then A-dam knew אֶת his wife again, and she gave birth to a son. And she called אֶת his name שֵׁת (*Shet*)

> *"For* שָׁת אֱלֹהִים *(Elohim has appointed) to me another child in the place of Ha-vel (Abel), because Ka-yin killed him."*

(26) And as for Shet, he also fathered a son, and he called אֶת his name E-nosh. At that time, he began to call on the name of יהוה (*YHVH*).

Chapter 5

Descendants of Adam

(1) This is the record of the generations of A-dam. When בָּרֹא אֱלֹהִים (*Elohim was creating*) A-dam בִּדְמוּת אֱלֹהִים (*in the likeness of Elohim*) עָשָׂה אֹתוֹ (*He made * him*).

(2) Male and female בְּרָאָם (*He created them*) וַיְבָרֶךְ אֹתָם (*and He blessed * them*) וַיִּקְרָא (*and He called*) אֶת their name אָדָם (*Adam*) when they were created.

(3-5) And when **A-dam** had lived a hundred and thirty years, he fathered a child in his likeness, according to his image. And he called אֶת his name Shet. And the days of A-dam after he fathered אֶת Shet were eight hundred years. And he fathered sons and daughters. And all the days of A-dam which he lived were nine hundred and thirty years, and he died.

(6-8) When **Shet** had lived a hundred and five years, he fathered אֶת E-nosh. And after Shet had fathered אֶת E-nosh he lived eight hundred and seven years, and fathered sons and daughters. And all the days of Shet were nine hundred and twelve years, and he died.

(9-11) When **E-nosh** lived ninety years, he fathered אֶת Kay-nan. And after E-nosh fathered אֶת Kay-nan he lived eight hundred and fifteen years, and fathered sons and daughters. And all the days of E-nosh were nine hundred and five years, and he died.

(12-14) When **Kay-nan** had lived seventy years, he fathered אֶת Ma-ha-lal-el. And after Kay-nan had fathered אֶת Ma-ha-lal-el, he lived eight hundred and forty

Level One   בְּרֵאשִׁית ~ ה

years, and fathered sons and daughters. And all the days of Kay-nan were nine hundred and ten years, and he died.

(15-17) When **Ma-ha-lal-el** had lived sixty-five years, he fathered אֶת Ya-red. And after Ma-ha-lal-el had fathered אֶת Ya-red, he lived eight hundred and thirty years, and fathered sons and daughters. And all the days of Ma-ha-lal-el were eight hundred and ninety-five years, and he died.

(18-20) When **Ya-red** had lived sixty-two and a hundred years, he fathered אֶת Kha-nokh (*Enoch*). And after Ya-red had fathered אֶת Kha-nokh (*Enoch*), he lived eight hundred years, and fathered sons and daughters. And all the days of Ya-red were nine hundred and sixty-two years, and he died.

(21-24) When **Kha-nokh** (*Enoch*) had lived sixty-five years, he fathered אֶת M'tu-she-lakh. And Kha-nokh (*Enoch*) walked with אֶת הָאֱלֹהִים (* *the Elohim*) after he fathered אֶת M'tu-she-lakh three hundred years, and fathered sons and daughters. And all the days of Kha-nokh (*Enoch*) were three hundred and sixty-five years. And Kha-nokh (*Enoch*) walked with אֶת הָאֱלֹהִים (* *the Elohim*) and he was no more כִּי-לָקַח אֹתוֹ אֱלֹהִים (*for Elohim took* him*).

(25-27) When **M'tu-she-lakh** had lived a hundred and eighty-seven years, he fathered אֶת La-mekh. And after M'tu-she-lakh had fathered אֶת La-mekh, he lived seven hundred and eighty-two years, and fathered sons and daughters. And all the days of M'tu-she-lakh were nine hundred and sixty-nine years, and he died.

(28) When **La-mekh** had lived a hundred and eighty-two years, he fathered a son.

(29) And he called אֶת his name נֹחַ (*Noah*), saying,

Genesis ~ 5

"This one יְנַחֲמֵנוּ (he shall console us) from our work, and from the hard labor of our hands, from the ground which אֲרָרָהּ יהוה (YHVH had cursed it)."

(30-31) And after La-mekh had fathered אֵת No-akh he lived five hundred and ninety-five years, and he fathered sons and daughters. All the days of La-mekh were seven hundred and seventy-seven years, and he died.

(32) When **No-akh** was five hundred years old, No-akh fathered אֵת Shem אֵת Kham וְאֵת (and *) Ya-fet (Japheth).

Chapter 6

Corruption Of The Human

(1) And it happened that, when the human began to multiply on the face of the ground, daughters were born to them.

(2) Then the sons of הָאֱלֹהִים (*the Elohim*) saw אֶת the daughters of the human, that they were טֹבֹת (*good ones*). And they took for themselves wives from all that they chose.

(3) וַיֹּאמֶר יהוה (*And YHVH said*)

לֹא־יָדוֹן רוּחִי
בָּאָדָם לְעֹלָם
בְּשַׁגַּם הוּא בָשָׂר
וְהָיוּ יָמָיו
מֵאָה וְעֶשְׂרִים שָׁנָה

My Spirit shall not govern
in the human forever
in that he is flesh,
and his days shall be
a hundred and twenty years.

(4) הַנְּפִלִים (*The N'fi-lim*) were upon the land in those days, and also afterward, when the sons of הָאֱלֹהִים (*the Elohim*) went into the daughters of the human, and they bore children to them.

Genesis ~ 6

(5) וַיַּרְא יהוה (*And YHVH saw*) that רַבָּה רָעַת (*much evil*) of the human was upon the land, and every inclination of the thoughts of his heart was only רַע (*evil*) every day.

(6) וַיִּנָּחֶם יהוה (*And YHVH regretted*) כִּי-עָשָׂה (*that He had made*) אֶת the human on the land וַיִּתְעַצֵּב (*and He grieved*) to His heart.

(7) וַיֹּאמֶר יהוה (*And YHVH said*)

אֶמְחֶה אֶת-הָאָדָם

אֲשֶׁר-בָּרָאתִי

מֵעַל פְּנֵי הָאֲדָמָה

I will wipe * the human
which I created
from on the face of the ground,

מֵאָדָם עַד-בְּהֵמָה

עַד-רֶמֶשׂ

וְעַד-עוֹף הַשָּׁמָיִם

כִּי נִחַמְתִּי כִּי עֲשִׂיתִם

from the human as far as animal,
as far as creeping thing,
and as far as the flyer of the sky,
because I regret that I made them.

(8) But No-akh found favor in the eyes of יהוה (*YHVH*).

Level One   בְּרֵאשִׁית ~ ו

Elohim Calls Noah

(9) These are the generations of No-akh. No-akh was a righteous man, without defect in his generations. No-akh walked with אֶת הָאֱלֹהִים (* the Elohim).

(10) And No-akh fathered three sons: אֵת Shem אֵת Kham וְאֶת (and *) Ya-fet (*Japheth*).

(11) And the land was corrupted before הָאֱלֹהִים (*the Elohim*) and the land was filled with violence.

(12) And אֱלֹהִים (*Elohim*) saw אֶת the land, and behold, it was corrupt, for all flesh had corrupted אֶת His way upon the land.

(13) And אֱלֹהִים (*Elohim*) said to No-akh,

קֵץ כָּל־בָּשָׂר

בָּא לְפָנַי

כִּי־מָלְאָה הָאָרֶץ חָמָס

מִפְּנֵיהֶם

וְהִנְנִי מַשְׁחִיתָם

אֶת־הָאָרֶץ

The end of all flesh
is coming to My face,
because the land is filled with cruelty
from their presence.
and behold, I am going to destroy them
*with * the land.*

(14)

עֲשֵׂה לְךָ תֵּבַת

עֲצֵי-גֹפֶר

קִנִּים תַּעֲשֶׂה אֶת-הַתֵּבָה

וְכָפַרְתָּ אֹתָהּ

מִבַּיִת וּמִחוּץ בַּכֹּפֶר

Make for yourself an ark of

woods of gopher;

*you shall make nests in * the ark,*

*and you must cover * her*

from inside and from outside in the covering.

(15)

וְזֶה אֲשֶׁר תַּעֲשֶׂה אֹתָהּ

שְׁלֹשׁ מֵאוֹת אַמָּה

אֹרֶךְ הַתֵּבָה

חֲמִשִּׁים אַמָּה רָחְבָּהּ

וּשְׁלֹשִׁים אַמָּה קוֹמָתָהּ

*And this is how you must make * her:*

three hundred cubits

the length of the ark;

fifty cubits - her width;

and thirty cubits - her height.

Level One

בְּרֵאשִׁית ~ ו

(16)

צֹהַר תַּעֲשֶׂה לַתֵּבָה

וְאֶל־אַמָּה תְּכַלֶנָּה מִלְמַעְלָה

וּפֶתַח הַתֵּבָה

בְּצִדָּהּ תָּשִׂים

תַּחְתִּיִּם שְׁנִיִּם

וּשְׁלִשִׁים תַּעֲשֶׂהָ

You must make a porthole for the ark,
and finish her to a cubit above.
And an opening of the ark
you shall place in her side.
Lower ones, second ones,
and third ones, you shall make her.

(17)

וַאֲנִי הִנְנִי מֵבִיא

אֶת־הַמַּבּוּל מַיִם עַל־הָאָרֶץ

לְשַׁחֵת כָּל־בָּשָׂר

אֲשֶׁר־בּוֹ רוּחַ חַיִּים

And I, behold, I am bringing
* the flood waters over the land
to destroy all flesh
in which is the breath of life

מִתַּחַת הַשָּׁמָיִם

כֹּל אֲשֶׁר-בָּאָרֶץ יִגְוָע

from under the sky;
everything that is on the land shall perish.

(18)

וַהֲקִמֹתִי

אֶת-בְּרִיתִי אִתָּךְ

וּבָאתָ אֶל-הַתֵּבָה

אַתָּה וּבָנֶיךָ וְאִשְׁתְּךָ

וּנְשֵׁי-בָנֶיךָ אִתָּךְ

And I will establish
* My covenant with * you,
and you must go into the ark
you, and your sons, and your wife,
and the wives of your sons with * you.

(19)

וּמִכָּל-הָחַי

מִכָּל-בָּשָׂר

And of every living thing,
from all flesh,

שְׁנַיִם מִכֹּל תָּבִיא אֶל-הַתֵּבָה

לְהַחֲיֹת אִתָּךְ

זָכָר וּנְקֵבָה יִהְיוּ

Level One   בְּרֵאשִׁית ~ ו

two from all you must bring into the ark

to keep them alive with * you;

they shall be male and female.

(20)

מֵהָעוֹף לְמִינֵהוּ

וּמִן־הַבְּהֵמָה לְמִינָהּ

מִכֹּל רֶמֶשׂ הָאֲדָמָה

לְמִינֵהוּ

שְׁנַיִם מִכֹּל

יָבֹאוּ אֵלֶיךָ לְהַחֲיוֹת

From the flyer for his species,

and from the cattle for her species,

from every creeping thing of the ground

for his species,

two from all

shall come to you to stay alive.

(21)

וְאַתָּה קַח־לְךָ

מִכָּל־מַאֲכָל אֲשֶׁר יֵאָכֵל

וְאָסַפְתָּ אֵלֶיךָ

And you, take for yourself

from all of food that is eaten,

and gather for yourself,

וְהָיָה לְךָ
וְלָהֶם לְאָכְלָה

and it shall be for you
and for them for food.

(22) And No-akh did according to all that צִוָּה אֹתוֹ אֱלֹהִים (*Elohim instructed * him*); thus he did.

Chapter 7

The Flood

(1) וַיֹּאמֶר יהוה *(And YHVH said)* to No-akh

בֹּא־אַתָּה וְכָל־בֵּיתְךָ

אֶל־הַתֵּבָה

כִּי־אֹתְךָ רָאִיתִי צַדִּיק

לְפָנַי בַּדּוֹר הַזֶּה

Go, you and all your household,

to the ark,

because I have seen * you are righteous

before Me in this generation.

(2) מִכֹּל הַבְּהֵמָה הַטְּהוֹרָה

תִּקַּח־לְךָ שִׁבְעָה שִׁבְעָה

אִישׁ וְאִשְׁתּוֹ

וּמִן־הַבְּהֵמָה אֲשֶׁר לֹא טְהֹרָה הִוא

שְׁנַיִם אִישׁ וְאִשְׁתּוֹ

From all the clean animal

you must take for yourself seven pairs,

a man and his woman;

and from the animal which is not clean,

two -- a man and his woman,

(3)

גַּם מֵעוֹף הַשָּׁמַיִם
שִׁבְעָה שִׁבְעָה
זָכָר וּנְקֵבָה
לְחַיּוֹת זֶרַע
עַל-פְּנֵי כָל-הָאָרֶץ

Also, from the flyer of the sky:

seven pairs,

male and female,

to keep alive seed

on the face of all the land.

(4)

כִּי לְיָמִים עוֹד שִׁבְעָה
אָנֹכִי מַמְטִיר עַל-הָאָרֶץ
אַרְבָּעִים יוֹם וְאַרְבָּעִים לָיְלָה
וּמָחִיתִי אֶת-כָּל-הַיְקוּם
אֲשֶׁר עָשִׂיתִי
מֵעַל פְּנֵי הָאֲדָמָה

Because for yet seven days

I will cause rain upon the land

for forty day and forty night.

*And I will wipe * all the living substance*

that I made

from upon the face of the ground.

Level One   בְּרֵאשִׁית ~ ז

(5) And No-akh did according to all that צִוָּהוּ יהוה (*YHVH instructed him*).

(6) No-akh was six hundred years old וְהַמַּבּוּל הָיָה מַיִם (*and the flood became waters*) on the land.

(7) And No-akh and his sons and his wife, and the wives of his sons with אִתּוֹ (* *him*), entered into הַתֵּבָה (*the ark*) because of מֵי הַמַּבּוּל (*the waters of the flood*).

(8) Of clean animal, and of animal which are not clean, and of the flyer, and all that creep upon the ground,

(9) two of each came to No-akh into הַתֵּבָה (*the ark*), male and female, as צִוָּה אֱלֹהִים (*Elohim instructed*) אֶת No-akh.

(10) And it happened that after seven days וּמֵי הַמַּבּוּל (*and the waters of the flood*) came over the land.

(11) In the six hundredth year of the life of No-akh, in the second month, on the seventeenth day of the month -- on that day all the springs of the great deep were split open, and the windows of the sky were opened.

(12) And הַגֶּשֶׁם (*the downpour*) came upon the land forty days and forty nights.

(13) On this same day, No-akh, Shem, Kham, and Ya-fet (*Japheth*), the sons of No-akh, and the wife of No-akh and the three wives of his sons with אִתָּם (* *them*), entered into הַתֵּבָה (*the ark*),

(14) they and every animal according to her kind, and every cattle according to her kind, and every creature that creeps upon the land according to his kind, and every flyer according to his kind, every bird of every wing.

(15) And they came to No-akh into הַתֵּבָה (*to the ark*) two of each, from every living thing in which was רוּחַ חַיִּים (*the breath of life*).

(16) And those that came, male and female, of every living thing, came as צִוָּה אֹתוֹ אֱלֹהִים (*Elohim had instructed* * *him*) וַיִּסְגֹּר יהוה (*And YHVH shut*) him in.

(17) And הַמַּבּוּל (*the flood*) came forty days and forty nights upon the land.

And הַמַּיִם (*the waters*) increased, and lifted אֶת-הַתֵּבָה (* *the ark*), and it rose up from the land.

(18) And הַמַּיִם (*the waters*) prevailed and increased greatly upon the land. And הַתֵּבָה (*the ark*) went upon the surface of הַמַּיִם (*the waters*).

(19) וְהַמַּיִם (*And the waters*) prevailed overwhelmingly upon the land, and they covered all the high mountains which were under the entire sky.

(20) הַמַּיִם (*The waters*) swelled fifteen cubits above the mountains, covering them.

(21) And every living thing that moved on the land perished -- in the flyer, and in the cattle, and in the animal, and in every creeper that creeps on the land, and in all the human.

(22) Everything in whose nostrils was רוּחַ חַיִּים (*the breath of life*), among all that was on dry land, died.

(23) וַיִּמַח (*And He wiped out*) אֵת every living substance upon the surface of the ground, from the human, to cattle, to creeper, and to the flyer of the sky; they were blotted out from the land. Only he remained, No-akh and those who were with אִתּוֹ (* *him*) בַּתֵּבָה (*in the ark*).

(24) And הַמַּיִם (*the waters*) prevailed over the land a hundred and fifty days.

Chapter 8

The Flood Abates

(1) וַיִּזְכֹּר אֱלֹהִים (*And Elohim remembered*) אֶת No-akh וְאֵת (*and **) every animal וְאֵת (*and **) every cattle that were with אִתּוֹ (** him*) בַּתֵּבָה (*in the ark*). וַיַּעֲבֵר אֱלֹהִים (*Elohim made*) רוּחַ (*a wind*) to blow over the land, and הַמָּיִם (*the waters*) subsided.

(2) And the fountains of the deep and the windows of the sky were closed, and הַגֶּשֶׁם (*the downpour*) from the sky was restrained.

(3) And הַמַּיִם (*the waters*) receded from the land gradually, and הַמַּיִם (*the waters*) abated at the end of a hundred and fifty days.

(4) And הַתֵּבָה (*the ark*) came to rest in the seventh month, on the seventeenth day of the month, on the mountains of A-ra-rat.

(5) וְהַמַּיִם (*And the waters*) continued to recede to the tenth month; in the tenth month, on the first of the month, the tops of the mountains appeared.

(6) And it happened that at the end of forty days No-akh opened אֶת the window of הַתֵּבָה (*the ark*) that he had made.

(7) And he sent out אֶת a raven; and it went to and fro until הַמַּיִם (*the waters*) were dried up from upon the land.

The Dove Is Sent Out

(8) And he sent out אֶת-הַיּוֹנָה (** the dove*) מֵאִתּוֹ (*from * him*) to see whether הַמַּיִם (*the waters*) had subsided from upon the ground.

(9) But הַיּוֹנָה (*the dove*) did not find a resting place for the sole of her foot, and she returned to him into הַתֵּבָה (*the ark*) for מַיִם (*the waters*) were still on the face

of the land. And he stretched out his hand and took her, and brought אֹתָהּ (* *her*) to himself into הַתֵּבָה (*the ark*).

(10) And he waited another seven days, and again he sent out אֶת-הַיּוֹנָה (* *the dove*) from הַתֵּבָה (*the ark*).

(11) And הַיּוֹנָה (*the dove*) came to him in the evening, and behold, a freshly-picked leaf of an olive tree was in her mouth. And No-akh knew that הַמַּיִם (*the waters*) had subsided from upon the land.

(12) And he waited seven more days, and he sent out אֶת-הַיּוֹנָה (* *the dove*). But she did not return again to him.

Leaving the Ark

(13) And it happened that, in the six hundred and first year, in the first month, on the first day of the month הַמַּיִם (*the waters*) dried up from upon the land. And No-akh removed אֵת the covering of הַתֵּבָה (*the ark*) and looked. And behold, the face of the ground was dried up.

(14) And in the second month, on the twenty-seventh day of the month, the land was dry.

(15) וַיְדַבֵּר אֱלֹהִים (*And Elohim spoke*) to No-akh לֵאמֹר (*saying*)

(16)

צֵא מִן-הַתֵּבָה

אַתָּה וְאִשְׁתְּךָ

וּבָנֶיךָ

וּנְשֵׁי-בָנֶיךָ אִתָּךְ

Level One   בְּרֵאשִׁית ~ ח

Come forth from the ark,

you, and your wife,

and your sons,

and the wives of your sons with * you.

(17)

כָּל־הַחַיָּה אֲשֶׁר־אִתְּךָ

מִכָּל־בָּשָׂר

בָּעוֹף וּבַבְּהֵמָה

וּבְכָל־הָרֶמֶשׂ הָרֹמֵשׂ עַל־הָאָרֶץ

הַיְצֵא אִתָּךְ

All the living that are with * you,

from all flesh,

in flyer, and in cattle,

and in all the creeper that creeps on the land,

bring forth with * you

וְשָׁרְצוּ בָאָרֶץ

וּפָרוּ וְרָבוּ עַל־הָאָרֶץ

and let them roam on the land

and be fruitful and increase on the land.

(18) So No-akh went out, with his sons and his wife, and the wives of his sons with אִתּוֹ (* him).

(19) Every animal, every creeping thing, and every flyer, and everything that

Genesis ~ 8

moves upon the land, according to their families, went out from הַתֵּבָה (*the ark*).

(20) And No-akh built an altar לַיהוה (*to YHVH*) and he took from all the clean animals and from all the clean flyer, and offered burnt offerings on the altar.

The Covenant with Noah

(21) וַיָּרַח יהוה (*And YHVH smelled*) the soothing אֶת fragrance, and וַיֹּאמֶר יהוה (*YHVH said*) to His heart

לֹא־אֹסִף
לֹא־אֹסִף לְקַלֵּל עוֹד
אֶת־הָאֲדָמָה בַּעֲבוּר הָאָדָם
כִּי יֵצֶר לֵב הָאָדָם
רַע מִנְּעֻרָיו
וְלֹא־אֹסִף עוֹד לְהַכּוֹת
אֶת־כָּל־חַי כַּאֲשֶׁר עָשִׂיתִי

I shall not continue to curse further
* the ground for the sake of the human,
because the form of the heart of the human
is evil from his youth.
And will I not continue to further punish
* all life as which I have done.

(22)

עֹד כָּל־יְמֵי הָאָרֶץ
זֶרַע וְקָצִיר וְקֹר וָחֹם

Level One   בְּרֵאשִׁית ~ ח

Furthermore, all the days of the land,
seed and harvest, and cold and heat,

וְקַיִץ וָחֹרֶף

וְיוֹם וָלַיְלָה

לֹא יִשְׁבֹּתוּ

and summer and winter,
and day and night,
they will not cease.

Chapter 9

Elohim Instructs Noah And His Sons

(1) וַיְבָרֶךְ אֱלֹהִים *(And Elohim blessed)* אֶת No-akh וְאֶת *(and *)* his sons וַיֹּאמֶר *(and He said)* to them,

פְּרוּ וּרְבוּ
וּמִלְאוּ אֶת־הָאָרֶץ

Be fruitful and increase,
and fill * the land.

(2)

וּמוֹרַאֲכֶם וְחִתְּכֶם
יִהְיֶה עַל כָּל־חַיַּת הָאָרֶץ
וְעַל כָּל־עוֹף הַשָּׁמָיִם
בְּכֹל אֲשֶׁר תִּרְמֹשׂ הָאֲדָמָה
וּבְכָל־דְּגֵי הַיָּם
בְּיֶדְכֶם נִתָּנוּ

And fear of you and dread of you
shall be in every life of the land,
and in every flyer of the sky,
and in all that creeps upon the ground,
and in all the fish of the sea,
in your hand they are given.

Level One   בְּרֵאשִׁית ~ ט

(3)

כָּל־רֶמֶשׂ אֲשֶׁר הוּא־חַי
לָכֶם יִהְיֶה לְאָכְלָה
כְּיֶרֶק עֵשֶׂב
נָתַתִּי לָכֶם אֶת־כֹּל

Every moving thing that lives,

for you, it shall be for food,

as the green plants,

*I give to you * all.*

(4)

אַךְ־בָּשָׂר בְּנַפְשׁוֹ
דָמוֹ לֹא תֹאכֵלוּ

Only the flesh on his soul,

his blood, you shall not eat.

(5)

וְאַךְ אֶת־דִּמְכֶם
לְנַפְשֹׁתֵיכֶם אֶדְרֹשׁ
מִיַּד כָּל־חַיָּה
אֶדְרְשֶׁנּוּ

*And yea, * the blood of you*

for your souls I require;

from the hand of all life,

I will require it.

49

וּמִיַּד הָאָדָם

מִיַּד אִישׁ אָחִיו

אֶדְרֹשׁ אֶת־נֶפֶשׁ הָאָדָם

And from the hand of the human,
from the hand of a man his brother,
*I will require * the soul of the human.*

(6)

שֹׁפֵךְ דַּם הָאָדָם

בָּאָדָם דָּמוֹ יִשָּׁפֵךְ

כִּי בְּצֶלֶם אֱלֹהִים

עָשָׂה אֶת־הָאָדָם

One shedding the blood of the human,
in the human, his blood shall be shed,
for in the image of Elohim
*He made * the human.*

(7)

וְאַתֶּם פְּרוּ וּרְבוּ

שִׁרְצוּ בָאָרֶץ וּרְבוּ־בָהּ

And you, be fruitful and increase,
roam on the land and increase on it.

(8) וַיֹּאמֶר אֱלֹהִים (*And Elohim said*) to No-akh and to his sons with אִתּוֹ (* him),

Level One   בְּרֵאשִׁית ~ ט

(9)

וַאֲנִי הִנְנִי מֵקִים

אֶת־בְּרִיתִי אִתְּכֶם

וְאֶת־זַרְעֲכֶם אַחֲרֵיכֶם

And I, behold, I am setting up
* My covenant with * you
and * your seed after you,

(10)

וְאֵת כָּל־נֶפֶשׁ הַחַיָּה

אֲשֶׁר אִתְּכֶם

בָּעוֹף בַּבְּהֵמָה

וּבְכָל־חַיַּת הָאָרֶץ אִתְּכֶם

מִכֹּל יֹצְאֵי הַתֵּבָה

לְכֹל חַיַּת הָאָרֶץ

and * every living soul
that is with * you,
in the flyer, in the animal,
and in all the life of the land with * you,
from all that came out of the ark
to all the life of the land.

(11)

וַהֲקִמֹתִי אֶת־בְּרִיתִי אִתְּכֶם

And I set up * My covenant with * you,

Genesis ~ 9

וְלֹא-יִכָּרֵת כָּל-בָּשָׂר עוֹד

מִמֵּי הַמַּבּוּל

וְלֹא-יִהְיֶה עוֹד מַבּוּל

לְשַׁחֵת הָאָרֶץ

and all flesh shall not be cut off again
from the waters of the flood,
and nor will there again be a flood
that destroys the land.

The Rainbow

(12) וַיֹּאמֶר אֱלֹהִים *(And Elohim said)*

זֹאת אוֹת-הַבְּרִית

אֲשֶׁר-אֲנִי נֹתֵן

בֵּינִי וּבֵינֵיכֶם

This is the sign of the covenant
that I am giving
between Me and you,

וּבֵין כָּל-נֶפֶשׁ חַיָּה

אֲשֶׁר אִתְּכֶם

לְדֹרֹת עוֹלָם

Level One   בְּרֵאשִׁית ~ ט

and between every soul living

that is with * you

for generations forever.

(13)

אֶת־קַשְׁתִּי נָתַתִּי בֶּעָנָן

וְהָיְתָה לְאוֹת

בְּרִית

בֵּינִי וּבֵין הָאָרֶץ

* My bow I give in the cloud,

and it shall be for a sign of

a covenant

between Me and the land.

(14)

וְהָיָה בְּעַנְנִי עָנָן

עַל־הָאָרֶץ

וְנִרְאֲתָה הַקֶּשֶׁת בֶּעָנָן

And it is when My cloud clouds

over the land

and the bow appears in the cloud.

(15)

וְזָכַרְתִּי

אֶת־בְּרִיתִי

And I will remember

* My covenant

Genesis ~ 9

אֲשֶׁר בֵּינִי וּבֵינֵיכֶם
וּבֵין כָּל־נֶפֶשׁ חַיָּה
בְּכָל־בָּשָׂר
וְלֹא־יִהְיֶה עוֹד
הַמַּיִם לְמַבּוּל
לְשַׁחֵת כָּל־בָּשָׂר

that is between Me and you,
and between every living soul
in all flesh.
And there will not be again
the waters for a flood
for the destruction of all flesh.

(16)

וְהָיְתָה הַקֶּשֶׁת בֶּעָנָן
וּרְאִיתִיהָ לִזְכֹּר
בְּרִית עוֹלָם

The bow shall be in the cloud,
and I will see it to remember
the everlasting covenant

בֵּין אֱלֹהִים
וּבֵין כָּל־נֶפֶשׁ חַיָּה
בְּכָל־בָּשָׂר אֲשֶׁר עַל־הָאָרֶץ

Level One בְּרֵאשִׁית ~ ט

> between Elohim
> and between every living soul,
> in all flesh that is on the land.

(17) וַיֹּאמֶר אֱלֹהִים *(And Elohim said)* to No-akh,

> זֹאת אוֹת־הַבְּרִית
> אֲשֶׁר הֲקִמֹתִי
> בֵּינִי וּבֵין כָּל־בָּשָׂר
> אֲשֶׁר עַל־הָאָרֶץ

> *This is the sign of the covenant*
> *which I set up*
> *is between Me and all flesh*
> *that is on the land.*

Noah's Sons

(18) Now the sons of No-akh who came out of the ark were Shem, Kham, and Ya-fet (Japheth). -- Kham was the father of K'na-an.

(19) These three were the sons of No-akh, and from these the whole land was populated.

Canaan Is Cursed

(20) And No-akh began to be a man of the ground, and he planted a vineyard.

(21) And he drank some of the wine and became drunk, and he exposed himself in the midst of his tent.

Genesis ~ 9

(22) And Kham, the father of K'na-an, saw אֵת the nakedness of his father, and he told his two brothers outside.

(23) Then Shem and Ya-fet (Japheth) took אֵת a garment, and the two of them put it on their shoulders and, walking backward, they covered אֵת the nakedness of their father. And their faces were turned backward, so that they did not see the nakedness of their father.

(24) Then No-akh awoke from his drunkenness, and he knew אֵת what his youngest son had done to him.

(25) And he said,

> "Cursed be K'na-an, a slave of servants he shall be to his brothers."

(26) Then he said,

> "Blessed be יהוה אֱלֹהֵי שֵׁם (YHVH, Elohim of Shem), and let K'na-an be a slave to them."

(27)

> "May אֱלֹהִים (Elohim) make space for Ya-fet (Japheth), and let him dwell in the tents of Shem, and let K'na-an be a slave for him."

Noah Dies

(28) And No-akh lived three hundred and fifty years after the flood.

(29) And all the days of No-akh were nine hundred and fifty years, and he died.

Chapter 10

Descendants Of Noah

(1) These are the generations of the sons of No-akh -- Shem, Kham, and Ya-fet (*Japheth*). Children were born to them after the flood.

(2) The sons of **Ya-fet** (*Japheth*): Go-mer, Ma-gog, Ma-dai, Ya-van, Tu-val, Me-shekh, and Ti-ras.

(3) And the sons of Go-mer: Ash-ka-naz, Ri-fat, and To-gar-mah.

(4) And the sons of Ya-van: E-li-shah, Tar-shish, Kit-tim, and Do-da-nim.

(5) From these the coastland peoples spread out through their lands, each according to his own language by their own families, in their nations.

(6) And the sons of **Kham**: Cush, Mitz-ra-yim, Put, and K'na-an.

(7) And the sons of Cush: S'va, Kha-vi-lah, Sav-tah, Ra-mah, and Sav-t'kha. The sons of Ra-mah: Sh'va and D'dan.

(8) And Cush fathered אֶת Nim-rod. He began to be a mighty one in the land.

(9) He was a mighty hunter before יהוה (*YHVH*). Therefore, it was said,

"Like Nim-rod a mighty hunter before יהוה (*YHVH*)."

(10-12) Now, the beginning of his kingdom was Ba-vel (Babylon), E-rekh, A-kad, and Khal-neh, in the land of Shin-ar. From that land he went out to A-shur, and he built אֶת Nin'veh וְאֶת (*and **) R'kho-vot City, וְאֶת (*and **) Ka-lakh, וְאֶת (*and **) Re-sen between Nin'veh and Ka-lakh; that is the great city.

(13-14) And **Mitz-ra-yim** fathered אֶת Lu-dim וְאֶת (*and **) A-na-mim וְאֶת (*and **) L'ha-vim וְאֶת (*and **) Naf-tu-khim וְאֶת (*and **) Pat-ru-sim וְאֶת (*and **)

Kas-lu-khim -- from there came P'lish-tim (*Philistines*) וְאֵת (*and **) Kaf-to-rim.

(15-18) **K'na-an** fathered אֵת Tzi-don, his firstborn וְאֵת (*and **) Khet וְאֵת (*and **) the Y'vu-si (*Jebusite*) וְאֵת (*and **) the E-mo-ri (*Amorite*) וְאֵת (*and **) the Gir-ga-shi (*Girgashite*) וְאֵת (*and **) the Khi-vi (*Hivite*) וְאֵת (*and **) the Ar-ki (*Arkite*) וְאֵת (*and **) the Si-ni (*Sinite*) וְאֵת (*and **) the Ar-va-ri (*Arvadite*) וְאֵת (*and **) the Tz'ma-ri (*Zemarite*) וְאֵת (*and **) the Kha-ma-ti (*Hamathite*). Afterward the families of the K'na-a-ni (*Canaanite*) were spread abroad.

(19) And the territory of the K'na-a-ni (*Canaanite*) was from Tzi-don (*Sidon*) in the direction of G'rar as far as A-zah, and in the direction of S'dom and A-mo-rah (*Gomorrah*), and Ad-mah, and Tz'vo-yim, as far as La-sha.

(20) These are the descendants of Kham, according to their families and their languages, in their lands, and in their nations.

(21-22) And to **Shem**, the father of all the children of E-ver, the older brother of Ya-fet (*Japheth*), children were also born. The sons of Shem: Ay-lam, A-shur, Ar-fakh-shad, Lud, and A-ram.

(23) And the sons of A-ram: Utz, and Khul, and Ge-ter, and Mash.

(24) And Ar-fakh-shad fathered אֵת Sha-lakh, and Sha-lakh fathered אֵת E-ver.

(25) And to E-ver two sons were born. The name of the one was Pe-leg, for in his days the land was divided, and the name of his brother was Yak-tan.

(26-29) And **Yak-tan** fathered אֵת Al-mo-dad וְאֵת (*and **) Sha-lef וְאֵת (*and **) Kha-tzar-ma-vet וְאֵת (*and **) Ya-rakh וְאֵת (*and **) Ha-do-ram וְאֵת (*and **) U-zal וְאֵת (*and **) Dik-lah וְאֵת (*and **) O-val וְאֵת (*and **) A-vi-ma-el וְאֵת (*and **) Sh'va וְאֵת (*and **) O-fir וְאֵת (*and **) Kha-vi-lah וְאֵת (*and **) Yo-vav. All these were the sons of Yak-tan.

Level One   בְּרֵאשִׁית ~ י

(30) And their dwelling place extended from Me-sha in the direction of S'far to the hill country of the east.

(31) These are the sons of Shem, according to their families, according to their languages, in their lands, and according to their nations.

(32) These are the families of the sons of No-akh, according to their generations and in their nations. And from these the nations spread abroad on the earth after the flood.

Chapter 11

Tower of Babel

(1) Now the whole land had one language and the same words.

(2) And as people migrated from the east they found a plain in the land of Shin-ar and settled there.

(3) And they said to each other,

> *"Come, let us make bricks and burn them thoroughly."*

And they had brick for stone and they had tar for mortar.

(4) And they said,

> *"Come, let us build ourselves a city and a tower whose top reaches to the sky. And let us make a name for ourselves, lest we be scattered over the face of the whole land."*

(5) Then יהוה (YHVH) came down to see אֶת the city וְאֶת (*and **) the tower that the sons of the human were building.

(6) וַיֹּאמֶר יהוה (*And YHVH said*)

הֵן עַם אֶחָד
וְשָׂפָה אַחַת לְכֻלָּם
וְזֶה הַחִלָּם לַעֲשׂוֹת

Behold, one people,
and one language for all of them,
and this is the start of what they do.

Level One
בְּרֵאשִׁית ~ יא

וְעַתָּה לֹא־יִבָּצֵר מֵהֶם

כֹּל אֲשֶׁר יָזְמוּ לַעֲשׂוֹת

And now nothing shall be restricted from them

of all that they are planning to do.

(7)

הָבָה נֵרְדָה

וְנָבְלָה שָׁם שְׂפָתָם

אֲשֶׁר לֹא יִשְׁמְעוּ

אִישׁ שְׂפַת רֵעֵהוּ

Come now, We will descend

and confuse their language there,

so that they will not hear

a man the language of his associate.

(8) וַיָּפֶץ יהוה (*And YHVH scattered*) אֹתָם (** them*) from there over the face of the whole land, and they stopped building the city.

(9) Therefore, its name was called Ba-vel (*Babylon*), for there בָּלַל יהוה (*YHVH mixed up*) the language of the whole land, and there הֱפִיצָם יהוה (*YHVH scattered*) them over the face of the whole land.

Descendants of Shem

(10-11) These are the generations of **Shem**. When Shem was a hundred years old, he fathered אֶת Ar-fakh-shad, two years after the flood. And Shem lived five hundred years after he fathered אֶת Ar-fakh-shad, and he fathered other sons and daughters.

Genesis ~ 11

(12-13) When **Ar-fakh-shad** had lived thirty-five years, he fathered אֵת Sha-lakh. And Ar-fakh-shad lived four hundred and three years after he fathered אֵת Sha-lakh, and he fathered other sons and daughters.

(14-15) When **Sha-lakh** had lived thirty years, he fathered אֵת E-ver. And Sha-lakh lived four hundred and three years after he fathered אֵת E-ver, and he fathered other sons and daughters.

(16-17) When **E-ver** had lived thirty-four years, he fathered אֵת Pe-leg. And E-ver lived four hundred and thirty years after he fathered אֵת Pe-leg, and he fathered other sons and daughters.

(18-19) When **Pe-leg** had lived thirty years, he fathered אֵת R'u. And Pe-leg lived two hundred and nine years after he fathered אֵת R'u, and he fathered other sons and daughters.

(20-21) When **R'u** had lived thirty-two years, he fathered אֵת S'rug. And R'u lived two hundred and seven years after he fathered אֵת S'rug, and he fathered other sons and daughters.

(22-23) When **S'rug** had lived thirty years, he fathered אֵת Na-khor. And S'rug lived two hundred years after he fathered אֵת Na-khor, and he fathered other sons and daughters.

(24-25) When **Na-khor** had lived twenty-nine years, he fathered אֵת Te-rakh. And Na-khor lived a hundred and nineteen years after he fathered אֵת Te-rakh, and he fathered other sons and daughters.

(26-27) When **Te-rakh** had lived seventy years, he fathered אֵת Av-ram, אֵת Na-khor, וְאֵת (*and* *) Ha-ran. Now these are the generations of Te-rakh. Te-rakh

Level One   בְּרֵאשִׁית ~ יא

fathered אֶת Av-ram אֶת Na-khor וְאֶת (*and* *) Ha-ran, and Ha-ran fathered אֶת Lot.

(28) And Ha-ran died in the presence of Te-rakh his father in the land of his birth, in Ur of the Kas-dim (*Chaldeans*).

(29) And Av-ram and Na-khor took wives for themselves. The name of the wife of Av-ram was Sa-rai, and the name of the wife of Na-khor was Mil-cah, the daughter of Ha-ran, the father of Mil-cah and the father of Yis-kah.

(30) And Sa-rai was barren; she had no child.

Terah Leaves Ur

(31-32) And Te-rakh took אֶת Av-ram his son וְאֶת (*and* *) Lot, the son of Ha-ran, his grandson וְאֶת (*and* *) Sa-rai his daughter-in-law, the wife of Av-ram his son, and went out with אֹתָם (* *them*) from Ur of Kas-dim (*Chaldeans*) to go to the land of K'na-an. And they went to Kha-ran, and they settled there. And the days of Te-rakh were two hundred and five years, and Te-rakh died in Kha-ran.

Chapter 12

Abram Sent From Ur

(1) וַיֹּאמֶר יהוה (*And YHVH said*) to Av-ram,

לֶךְ־לְךָ מֵאַרְצְךָ

וּמִמּוֹלַדְתְּךָ

וּמִבֵּית אָבִיךָ

אֶל־הָאָרֶץ

אֲשֶׁר אַרְאֶךָּ

Go for yourself from your land
and from your kindred,
and from the house of your father,
to the land
that I will show you.

(2)

וְאֶעֶשְׂךָ לְגוֹי גָּדוֹל

וַאֲבָרֶכְךָ

וַאֲגַדְּלָה שְׁמֶךָ

וֶהְיֵה בְּרָכָה

And I will make you a great nation,
and I will bless you,
and I will make your name great,
and you will be a blessing.

Level One

בְּרֵאשִׁית ~ יב

(3)

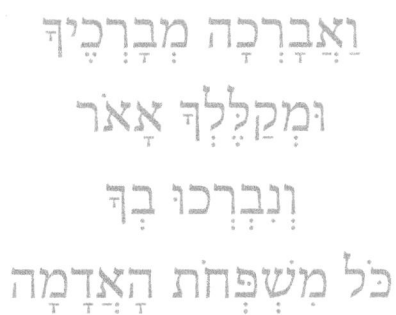

וַאֲבָרְכָה מְבָרְכֶיךָ
וּמְקַלֶּלְךָ אָאֹר
וְנִבְרְכוּ בְךָ
כֹּל מִשְׁפְּחֹת הָאֲדָמָה

And I will bless the ones who bless you,
and one making light of you, I will curse.
And they will be blessed in you --
all families of the ground.

Abram Obeys

(4) And Av-ram went out as דִּבֶּר יהוה (*YHVH told*) to him, and Lot went with אִתּוֹ (** him*). Now Av-ram was seventy-five years old when he went out from Kha-ran.

(5) And Av-ram took אֵת Sa-rai his wife וְאֵת (*and **) Lot his nephew וְאֵת (*and **) all their possessions that they had gathered וְאֵת (*and **) all the persons that they had acquired in Kha-ran, and they went out to go to the land of K'na-an. And they went to the land of K'na-an.

(6) And Av-ram traveled through the land up to the place of Sh'khem, to the Oak of Mo-reh. And the K'na-a-ni (*Canaanite*) were in the land at that time.

(7) וַיֵּרָא יהוה (*And YHVH appeared*) to Av-ram וַיֹּאמֶר (*and He said*)

לְזַרְעֲךָ אֶתֵּן אֶת-הָאָרֶץ הַזֹּאת

To your seed I will give * this land.

And he built an altar there לַיהוה (*to YHVH*) Who had appeared to him.

(8) And he moved on from there to the hill country, east לְבֵית-אֵל (*to Bet-El / the house of El*). And he pitched his tent at בֵּית-אֵל (*Bet-El / the house of El*) on the west, and at the Ai on the east. And he built an altar there לַיהוה (*to YHVH*). And he called on the name of יהוה (*YHVH*).

(9) And Av-ram kept moving on, toward the Ne-gev.

Abram Goes to Egypt

(10) And there was a famine in the land. And Av-ram went down to Mitz-ra-yim (*Egypt*) to sojourn there, for the famine was severe in the land.

(11) And it happened that as he drew near to enter into Mitz-ra-yim (*Egypt*), he said to Sa-rai his wife,

> "Look now, I know that אַתְּ (*you*) are a woman beautiful of appearance"

(12)

> "And it shall happen that, if the Mitz-rim (*Egyptians*) see אֹתָךְ (* *you*), then they will say,
>
> 'This is his wife.' "
>
> "And they will kill אֹתִי (* *me*) וְאֹתָךְ (*and * you*) they will keep alive."

(13)

> "Please say אַתְּ (*you*) are my sister so that it will go well for me on your account. Then I will live on account of you."

(14) And it happened that as Av-ram came into Mitz-ra-yim (*Egypt*), the

Mitz-rim (*Egyptians*) saw אֵת the woman, that she was very beautiful.

(15) And the officials of Far-oh saw אֹתָה (* *her*), and they praised אֹתָה (* *her*) beauty to Far-oh. And the woman was taken to the house of Far-oh.

(16) And he dealt well with Av-ram on account of her, and he had sheep, cattle, male donkeys, male servants, female servants, female donkeys, and camels.

(17) וַיְנַגַּע יהוה (*And YHVH afflicted*) אֶת Far-oh וְאֶת (*and* *) his household with severe plagues on account of the matter of Sa-rai the wife of Av-ram.

(18) Then Far-oh called for Av-ram and said,

> *"What is this you have done to me? Why did you not tell me that she was your wife?"*

(19)

> *"Why did you say,*
>
>> *'She is my sister?'*
>
> *"And I took* אֹתָה *(* *her) to myself as a wife. Now here is your wife. Take her and go."*

(20) And Far-oh commanded his men concerning him, and then sent אֹתוֹ (* *him*) וְאֶת (*and* *) his wife וְאֶת (*and* *) all that was with him away.

Chapter 13

Abram Leaves Egypt

(1) Then Av-ram went up from Mitz-ra-yim (Egypt), he and his wife and all that was with him. And Lot went with him to the Ne-gev.

(2) And Av-ram was very wealthy in livestock, in silver, and in gold.

(3) And he went according to his journey from Ne-gev, then to בֵּית-אֵל (Bet-El / the house of El), to the place where his tent was at the beginning, between בֵּית-אֵל (Bet-El / the house of El) and Ai,

(4) to the place where he had made an altar at the beginning. And Av-ram called on the name of יהוה (YHVH) there.

Abram and Lot Separate

(5) And also Lot, who went with אֶת Av-ram, had herds and tents.

(6) And the land could not support אֹתָם (* them) so as to live together, because their possessions were so many that they were not able to live together.

(7) And there was a quarrel between רֹעֵי (the shepherds of) the livestock of Av-ram and רֹעֵי (the shepherds of) the livestock of Lot. And the K'na-a-ni (Canaanite) and the P'ri-zi (Perizzite) were living in the land.

(8) Then Av-ram said to Lot,

> "Please, let there not be quarreling between me and you, and between רֹעַי (my shepherds) and your shepherds, for we are men -- brothers."

(19)

> "Is not the whole land before you? Separate yourself from me. If

Level One

בְּרֵאשִׁית ~ יג

you want what is on the left, then I will go right; if you want what is on the right, I will go left."

(10) And Lot lifted up אֶת his eyes and saw אֶת the whole plain of the Yar-den (Jordan), that all of it was well-watered land -- this was before שִׁחֵת יהוה (*YHVH destroyed*) אֶת S'dom וְאֶת (*and **) A-mo-rah (*Gomorrah*) -- like the Garden of יהוה (*YHVH*) like the land of Mitz-ra-yim (*Egypt*) in the direction of Zo-ar.

(11) So Lot chose for himself אֵת all the plain of the Yar-den (*Jordan*). And Lot journeyed from the east, and so they separated from each other.

(12) Av-ram settled in the land of K'na-an, and Lot settled in the cities of the plain. And he pitched his tent as far as S'dom.

(13) Now the men of S'dom were רָעִים (*evil ones*) and sinners לַיהוה (*to YHVH*).

Abram is Promised The Land

(14) וַיהוה (*And YHVH*) said to Av-ram after Lot had separated from him,

שָׂא נָא עֵינֶיךָ

וּרְאֵה מִן-הַמָּקוֹם

אֲשֶׁר-אַתָּה שָׁם

צָפֹנָה וָנֶגְבָּה

וָקֵדְמָה וָיָמָּה

Please, lift up your eyes

and see from the place

there which you are

northward and southward

and eastward and seaward.

(15)

כִּי אֶת־כָּל־הָאָרֶץ

אֲשֶׁר־אַתָּה רֹאֶה

לְךָ אֶתְּנֶנָּה

וּלְזַרְעֲךָ עַד־עוֹלָם

Because * all the land
which you see
I will give to you,
and to your seed forever.

(16)

וְשַׂמְתִּי אֶת־זַרְעֲךָ

כַּעֲפַר הָאָרֶץ

אֲשֶׁר אִם־יוּכַל אִישׁ

לִמְנוֹת אֶת־עֲפַר הָאָרֶץ

גַּם־זַרְעֲךָ יִמָּנֶה

I will place * your seed
like the soil of the land
which if a man is able
to number * the soil of the land,
also, your seed shall be numbered.

(17)

קוּם הִתְהַלֵּךְ בָּאָרֶץ

לְאָרְכָּהּ וּלְרָחְבָּהּ

כִּי לְךָ אֶתְּנֶנָּה

Level One

בְּרֵאשִׁית ~ יג

Arise, walk in the land
to its length and to its width,
because I am giving it to you.

(18) So Av-ram pitched his tent, and he came and settled at the oaks of Mam-re, which were at Hev-ron. And there he built an altar לַיהוה (*to YHVH*).

Chapter 14

War of the Kings

(1) And it happened that in the days of Am-ra-fel, the king of Shin-ar, Ar-yokh, the king of El-la-sar, K'dar-la-o-mer, the king of E-lam, and Tid-al, the king of nations,

(2) made war with אֶת־בֶּרַע (*Bera/ in evil*), the king of S'dom וְאֶת (*and *) Bir-sha, the king of A-mo-rah (*Gomorrah*), Shin-av, the king of Ad-mah, and Shem-E-ver, the king of Tz'vo-yim, and the king of Be-la -- that is, Zo-ar.

(3) All these joined forces at the valley of the Sid-dim -- that is, the sea of the salt.

(4) Twelve years they had served אֶת K'dar-la-o-mer, but in the thirteenth year they rebelled.

(5-6) In the fourteenth year K'dar-la-o-mer and the kings who were with אִתּוֹ (* *him*) came and defeated אֶת R'fa-im in Ash-t'rot~Kar-na-yim וְאֶת (*and *) the Zu-zim in Ham וְאֵת (*and *) the E-mim in Sha-veh Kir-ya-ta-yim וְאֵת (*and *) the Kho-ri (*Horites*) in their hill country of Se-ir, as far as El~Pa-ran, which is at the wilderness.

(7) Then they turned back and came to En~Mish-pat -- that is, Ka-desh. And they defeated אֵת the whole field of the A-ma-le-ki (*Amalekites*), and also אֶת the E-mo-ri (*Amorites*) who were dwelling in Kha-tzon~Ta-mar.

(8) Then the king of S'dom, the king of A-mo-rah (*Gomorrah*), the king of Ad-mah, the king of Tz'vo-yim, and the king of Be-la -- that is Zo-ar, went out, and they took up battle position with אִתָּם (* *them*) in the Valley of Sid-dim –

(9) אֵת K'dar-la-o-mer, king of E-lam, and Tid-al, king of nations, and Am-ra-fel, king of Shin-ar, and Ar-yokh, king of El-la-sar, four kings against אֶת five.

Level One   בְּרֵאשִׁית ~ יד

(10) Now the Valley of Sid-dim was full of tar pits. And the kings of S'dom and A-mo-rah (*Gomorrah*) fled and fell into them, but the rest fled to the mountains.

(11) So they took אֶת all the possessions of S'dom and A-mo-rah (*Gomorrah*) וְאֶת (*and **) all their provisions, and they left.

(12) And they took אֶת Lot, the son of the brother of Av-ram וְאֶת (*and **) his possessions, and left. Now he had been dwelling in S'dom.

(13) Then one who escaped came and told Av-ram the Iv-ri (*Hebrew*). And he was living at the oaks of Mam-re the E-mo-ri (*Amorite*), brother of Esh-kol and brother of A-ner. They were allies with Av-ram.

Abram Goes To War

(14) When Av-ram heard that his relative was taken captive, he summoned אֶת his trained men, born in his house, three hundred and eighteen of them, and he went in pursuit up to Dan.

(15) And he divided his trained men against them at night, he and his servants. And he defeated them and pursued them to Ho-vah, which is north of Da-me-sek.

(16) And he brought back אֶת all the possessions. And he also brought back אֶת Lot, his relative, and his possessions, and אֶת the women וְאֶת (*and **) the people as well.

(17) And the king of S'dom went out to meet him after his return from defeating אֶת K'dar-la-o-mer וְאֶת (*and **) the kings who were with אִתּוֹ (** him*), to the Valley of Sha-veh -- that is, the Valley of the King.

The King of Righteousness

(18) וּמַלְכִּי-צֶדֶק (*And* Mal-ki~Tze-dek /*the king of righteousness*) the king of Sha-lem, brought out bread and wine. He was the priest לְאֵל עֶלְיוֹן (*to El Most High*).

Genesis ~ 14

(19) And he blessed him and said,

> "Blessed be Av-ram לְאֵל עֶלְיוֹן (for El Most High) קֹנֵה שָׁמַיִם וָאָרֶץ (Creator of sky and land)."

(20)

> "And blessed be אֵל עֶלְיוֹן (El Most High) Who delivered your enemies into your hand."

And he gave to him a tenth of everything.

Abram Refuses The Spoil

(21) And the king of S'dom said to Av-ram,

> "Give me the people, but the possessions take for yourself."

(22) And Av-ram said to the king of S'dom,

> "I have raised my hand to יהוה אֵל עֶלְיוֹן (YHVH, El Most High) קֹנֵה שָׁמַיִם וָאָרֶץ (Creator of sky and land)."

(23)

> "I will not take from a thread to a lacing of a sandal from all that belongs to you. You shall not say,
>
>> 'I made אֶת Av-ram rich.'"

(24)

> "Nothing besides what the young men have eaten and the share of the men who went out with אִתִּי (* me) will I take. A-ner, Esh-kol, and Mam-re, they shall take their share."

Chapter 15

Abram Promised A Son

(1) After these things הָיָה דְבַר־יהוה (*the word of YHVH was*) to Av-ram in a vision לֵאמֹר (*saying*)

אַל־תִּירָא אַבְרָם

אָנֹכִי מָגֵן לָךְ

שְׂכָרְךָ הַרְבֵּה מְאֹד

Do not be afraid, Av-ram;
I am a shield to you,
your reward shall increase much.

(2) Then Av-ram said,

> אֲדֹנָי יהוה (*My Lord YHVH*) what will You give me? I continue to be childless, and my heir is E-li-e-zer of Da-me-sek."

(3) And Av-ram said,

> "Look, You have not given me a descendant, and behold, a son of my household will succeed אֹתִי (* *me*)."

(4) And behold דְבַר־יהוה (*the word of YHVH*) to him לֵאמֹר (*saying*)

לֹא יִירָשְׁךָ זֶה

This one will not be your heir,

Genesis ~ 15

כִּי-אִם אֲשֶׁר יֵצֵא

מִמֵּעֶיךָ

הוּא יִירָשֶׁךָ

but rather he who comes forth

from your bowels,

he shall be your heir.

(5) וַיּוֹצֵא אֹתוֹ (*And He brought * him*) outside וַיֹּאמֶר (*and He said*)

הַבֶּט-נָא הַשָּׁמַיְמָה

וּסְפֹר הַכּוֹכָבִים

אִם-תּוּכַל לִסְפֹּר אֹתָם

כֹּה יִהְיֶה זַרְעֶךָ

Look toward the sky, please

and count the stars

*if you are able to count * them.*

And He said to him,

Thus shall your seed be.

(6) And he believed בַּיהוה (*on YHVH*) וַיַּחְשְׁבֶהָ (*and He reckoned it*) to him as righteousness.

The Covenant

(7) וַיֹּאמֶר (*And He said*) to him,

Level One   בְּרֵאשִׁית ~ טו

אֲנִי יהוה

אֲשֶׁר הוֹצֵאתִיךָ

מֵאוּר כַּשְׂדִּים

לָתֶת לְךָ

אֶת-הָאָרֶץ הַזֹּאת

לְרִשְׁתָּהּ

I am YHVH

Who brought you forth

from Ur of the Kas-dim

to give to you

* this land

to inherit it.

(8) And he said,

אֲדֹנָי יהוה (*My Lord YHVH*) *how shall I know that I will possess it?"*

(9) וַיֹּאמֶר (*And He said*) *to him,*

קְחָה לִי עֶגְלָה מְשֻׁלֶּשֶׁת

וְעֵז מְשֻׁלֶּשֶׁת

Take for Me a three-year-old heifer,

and a three-year-old goat,

וְאַיִל מְשֻׁלָּשׁ
וְתֹר וְגוֹזָל

and a three-year-old ram,
and a dove and a nestling.

(10) And he took for Him אֶת *all these and cut* אֹתָם (* *them*) *in pieces down the middle. And he put each piece opposite the other* וְאֶת (*and* *) *the bird he did not cut.*

(11) And the birds of prey came down on the carcasses, but Av-ram drove אֹתָם (* *them*) away.

(12) And it happened, as the sun went down, then a deep sleep fell upon Av-ram and, behold, a great terrifying darkness fell upon him.

(13) וַיֹּאמֶר לְאַבְרָם (*And He said to Av-ram*)

יָדֹעַ תֵּדַע
כִּי־גֵר יִהְיֶה זַרְעֲךָ
בְּאֶרֶץ לֹא לָהֶם

Know that you know
that your seed shall be a stranger
in a land not for them.

וַעֲבָדוּם
וְעִנּוּ אֹתָם
אַרְבַּע מֵאוֹת שָׁנָה

Level One בְּרֵאשִׁית ~ טו

And they shall serve them
and they shall oppress * them
four hundred years.

(14)

וְגַם אֶת־הַגּוֹי

אֲשֶׁר יַעֲבֹדוּ

דָּן אָנֹכִי

וְאַחֲרֵי־כֵן יֵצְאוּ

בִּרְכֻשׁ גָּדוֹל

And also * the nation
that they serve
I will judge,
and afterward they shall come forth
in great possessions.

(15)

וְאַתָּה תָּבוֹא

אֶל־אֲבֹתֶיךָ בְּשָׁלוֹם

תִּקָּבֵר בְּשֵׂיבָה טוֹבָה

And you, you shall come
to your fathers in peace;
you shall be buried in a good old age.

(16)

וְדוֹר רְבִיעִי יָשׁוּבוּ הֵנָּה

And the fourth generation shall return here,

Genesis ~ 15

כִּי לֹא־שָׁלֵם עֲוֹן הָאֱמֹרִי עַד־הֵנָּה

for the sin of the Amorite is not yet complete.

(17) And after the sun had gone down and it was dusk, behold, a smoking firepot and a flaming torch passed between those half pieces.

(18) On that day כָּרַת יהוה (*YHVH cut*) בְּרִית (*a covenant*) with אֶת Av-ram לֵאמֹר (*saying*)

לְזַרְעֲךָ נָתַתִּי

אֶת־הָאָרֶץ הַזֹּאת

מִנְּהַר מִצְרַיִם

עַד־הַנָּהָר הַגָּדֹל

נְהַר־פְּרָת

To your seed I will give
* this land
from the river of Egypt
as far as the great river,
the river of P'rat,

(19)

אֶת־הַקֵּינִי

וְאֶת־הַקְּנִזִּי

וְאֵת הַקַּדְמֹנִי

* the Kenite,
and * the Kenizzite,
and * the Kadmonite,

Level One

בְּרֵאשִׁית ~ טו

(20)

וְאֶת־הַחִתִּי

וְאֶת־הַפְּרִזִּי

וְאֶת־הָרְפָאִים

and * the Hittite,
and * the Perizzite,
and * the Rephaim,

(21)

וְאֶת־הָאֱמֹרִי

וְאֶת־הַכְּנַעֲנִי

וְאֶת־הַגִּרְגָּשִׁי

וְאֶת־הַיְבוּסִי

and * the Amorite,
and * the Canaanite,
and * the Girgashite,
and * the Jebusite.

Chapter 16

Hagar Conceives

(1) Now Sa-rai, the wife of Av-ram, had borne him no children. And she had a female Mitz-rit (*Egyptian*) servant, and her name was Ha-gar.

(2) And Sa-rai said to Av-ram,

> "Look, please עֲצָרַנִי יהוה (*YHVH has restrained*) *me from bearing children. Please go in to my servant; perhaps I will have children by her.*"

And Av-ram listened to the voice of Sa-rai.

(3) Then Sa-rai, the wife of Av-ram, took אֵת Ha-gar, her Mitz-rit (*Egyptian*) servant, after Av-ram had lived ten years in the land of K'na-an, and gave אֹתָהּ (**her*) to Av-ram her husband as his wife.

(4) And he went in to Ha-gar, and she conceived. And when she saw that she had conceived, then her mistress grew small in her eyes.

Sarai And Hagar At Odds

(5) And Sa-rai said to Av-ram,

> "*My wrong be upon you. I had my servant sleep with you, and when she saw that she had conceived, she no longer respected me.* יִשְׁפֹּט יהוה (*May YHVH judge*) *between me and you!*"

(6) And Av-ram said to Sa-rai,

> "*Look, your servant is under your authority. Do to her* הַטּוֹב (*the*

Level One   בְּרֵאשִׁית ~ טז

good) in your eyes."

And Sa-rai mistreated her, and she fled from her presence.

Ishmael Is Born

(7) וַיִּמְצָאָהּ מַלְאַךְ יהוה (*And the messenger of YHVH found her*) at a spring of water in the wilderness, at the spring by the road of Shur.

(8) וַיֹּאמֶר (*And He said*) to Ha-gar, the servant of Sa-rai,

אֵי־מִזֶּה בָאת

וְאָנָה תֵלֵכִי

> *From where have you come,*
> *and where are you going?*

And she said,

> *"I am fleeing from the presence of Sa-rai my mistress."*

(9) וַיֹּאמֶר לָהּ מַלְאַךְ יהוה (*And the messenger of YHVH said to her*)

שׁוּבִי אֶל־גְּבִרְתֵּךְ

וְהִתְעַנִּי

תַּחַת יָדֶיהָ

> *Return to your mistress*
> *and humble yourself*
> *under her hands.*

(10) וַיֹּאמֶר לָהּ מַלְאַךְ יהוה (*And the messenger of YHVH said to her*)

Genesis ~ 16

הַרְבָּה אַרְבֶּה אֶת־זַרְעֵךְ

וְלֹא יִסָּפֵר מֵרֹב

I will greatly increase * your seed,

and he shall not be counted from abundance.

(11) וַיֹּאמֶר לָהּ מַלְאַךְ יהוה (*And the messenger of YHVH said to her*)

הִנָּךְ הָרָה

וְיֹלַדְתְּ בֵּן

וְקָרָאת שְׁמוֹ יִשְׁמָעֵאל

כִּי־שָׁמַע יהוה

אֶל־עָנְיֵךְ

Behold, you are pregnant

and shall give birth to a son.

And you shall call his name Yish-ma-el,

because YHVH has listened

to your suffering.

(12)

וְהוּא יִהְיֶה פֶּרֶא אָדָם

יָדוֹ בַכֹּל

וְיַד כֹּל בּוֹ

וְעַל־פְּנֵי כָל־אֶחָיו יִשְׁכֹּן

Level One

בְּרֵאשִׁית ~ טז

And he shall be a wild donkey of a human,

his hand on all

and the hand of all on him,

and he will dwell in the presence all his brothers.

(13) So she called the name of יהוה (*YHVH*) Who spoke to her אַתָּה (*You are*) אֵל רֳאִי (*El Who sees me*) for she said,

"Here I have seen after רֳאִי (the One who sees me)."

(14) Therefore, the well was called בְּאֵר לַחַי רֹאִי (B'er~La-khai~Ro-i); behold, it is between Ka-desh and Ba-red.

(15) And Ha-gar had a child for Av-ram, a son. And Av-ram called the name of his son whom Ha-gar bore to him, Yish-ma-el.

(16) And Av-ram was eighty-six years old when Ha-gar bore אֶת Yish-ma-el to Av-ram.

Chapter 17

Abram To Abraham

(1) When Av-ram was ninety-nine years old וַיֵּרָא יהוה (*YHVH appeared*) to Av-ram. וַיֹּאמֶר (*And He said*) to him,

אֲנִי־אֵל שַׁדַּי
הִתְהַלֵּךְ לְפָנַי
וֶהְיֵה תָמִים

I am El Almighty
walk before Me
and be flawless.

(2)

וְאֶתְּנָה בְרִיתִי
בֵּינִי וּבֵינֶךָ
וְאַרְבֶּה אוֹתְךָ
בִּמְאֹד מְאֹד

And I am giving My covenant
between Me and you,
*and I will increase * you*
very much.

(3) Then Av-ram fell upon his face and וַיְדַבֵּר אִתּוֹ אֱלֹהִים (*Elohim spoke with * him*) לֵאמֹר (*saying*):

Level One בְּרֵאשִׁית ~ יז

(4)

אֲנִי הִנֵּה בְרִיתִי אִתָּךְ
וְהָיִיתָ לְאַב
הֲמוֹן גּוֹיִם

I behold My covenant with * you,
and you shall be for a father
of a multitude of nations.

(5)

וְלֹא־יִקָּרֵא עוֹד
אֶת־שִׁמְךָ אַבְרָם
וְהָיָה שִׁמְךָ אַבְרָהָם
כִּי אַב־הֲמוֹן גּוֹיִם
נְתַתִּיךָ

And it shall not be called again
* Your name Abram,
but your name shall be Abraham,
because a father of a multitude of nations
I give you.

(6)

וְהִפְרֵתִי אֹתְךָ
בִּמְאֹד מְאֹד

And I will make * you fruitful
in much excess.

Genesis ~ 17

וּנְתַתִּיךָ לְגוֹיִם
וּמְלָכִים מִמְּךָ יֵצֵאוּ

*I appoint you to nations,
and kings shall come forth from you.*

(7)

וַהֲקִמֹתִי אֶת־בְּרִיתִי
בֵּינִי וּבֵינֶךָ
וּבֵין זַרְעֲךָ אַחֲרֶיךָ
לְדֹרֹתָם

*And I set up * My covenant
between Me and between you,
and between your seed after you,
for their generations*

לִבְרִית עוֹלָם
לִהְיוֹת לְךָ לֵאלֹהִים
וּלְזַרְעֲךָ אַחֲרֶיךָ

*for a covenant forever
to be to you for an Elohim
and to your seed after you.*

(8)

וְנָתַתִּי לְךָ וּלְזַרְעֲךָ אַחֲרֶיךָ

And I will give to you and to your seed after you

Level One

בְּרֵאשִׁית ~ יז

אֵת אֶרֶץ מְגֻרֶיךָ
אֵת כָּל-אֶרֶץ כְּנַעַן
לַאֲחֻזַּת עוֹלָם
וְהָיִיתִי לָהֶם לֵאלֹהִים

* the land of your sojournings,

* all the land of K'na-an,

for holding forever,

and I will be to them for an Elohim.

(9) וַיֹּאמֶר אֱלֹהִים (And Elohim said) to Av-ra-ham,

וְאַתָּה אֶת-בְּרִיתִי תִשְׁמֹר
אַתָּה וְזַרְעֲךָ אַחֲרֶיךָ
לְדֹרֹתָם

And you, you must guard * My covenant,

you and your seed after you,

for their generations.

Covenant of Circumcision

(10)

זֹאת בְּרִיתִי אֲשֶׁר תִּשְׁמְרוּ

This is My covenant which you shall guard,

Genesis ~ 17

בֵּינִי וּבֵינֵיכֶם

וּבֵין זַרְעֲךָ אַחֲרֶיךָ

הִמּוֹל לָכֶם כָּל-זָכָר

between Me and you,
and between your seed after you:
Every male for you shall be circumcised.

(11)

וּנְמַלְתֶּם

אֵת בְּשַׂר עָרְלַתְכֶם

וְהָיָה לְאוֹת בְּרִית

בֵּינִי וּבֵינֵיכֶם

And you shall circumcise
* the flesh of your foreskin,
and it is for a sign of a covenant
between Me and you.

(12)

וּבֶן-שְׁמֹנַת יָמִים

יִמּוֹל לָכֶם

כָּל-זָכָר

לְדֹרֹתֵיכֶם

And a son of eight days
shall be circumcised for you,
every male
for your generations,

Level One   בְּרֵאשִׁית ~ יז

יְלִיד בָּיִת

וּמִקְנַת־כֶּסֶף

מִכֹּל בֶּן־נֵכָר

אֲשֶׁר לֹא מִזַּרְעֲךָ הוּא

one born of house

and one acquired of silver

from every son of a foreigner

who he is not from your seed.

(13)

הִמּוֹל יִמּוֹל

יְלִיד בֵּיתְךָ

וּמִקְנַת כַּסְפֶּךָ

וְהָיְתָה בְרִיתִי בִּבְשַׂרְכֶם

לִבְרִית עוֹלָם

To be circumcised he shall be circumcised

is one who is born in your house

and acquired of your silver.

And it is My covenant in your flesh

for a covenant forever.

(14)

וְעָרֵל זָכָר

אֲשֶׁר לֹא־יִמּוֹל

And an uncircumcised male

who has not circumcised

אֶת-בְּשַׂר עָרְלָתוֹ

וְנִכְרְתָה הַנֶּפֶשׁ הַהִוא

מֵעַמֶּיהָ

אֶת-בְּרִיתִי הֵפַר

the flesh of his foreskin

then that soul shall be cut off

from his people.

*He has annulled * My covenant.*

Sarai To Sarah

(15) וַיֹּאמֶר אֱלֹהִים (*And Elohim said*) to Av-ra-ham,

שָׂרַי אִשְׁתְּךָ

לֹא-תִקְרָא אֶת-שְׁמָהּ שָׂרָי

כִּי שָׂרָה שְׁמָהּ

Sarai your wife,

*you shall not call * her name Sarai,*

because Sarah will be her name.

Isaac Is Promised

(16)

וּבֵרַכְתִּי אֹתָהּ

וְגַם נָתַתִּי מִמֶּנָּה

לְךָ בֵּן

Level One

בְּרֵאשִׁית ~ יז

And I will bless * her;
and also, I give from her
to you a son.

וּבֵרַכְתִּיהָ

וְהָיְתָה לְגוֹיִם

מַלְכֵי עַמִּים

מִמֶּנָּה יִהְיוּ

And I will bless her,
and she is for nations.
Kings of peoples
shall come from her.

(17) And Av-ra-ham fell upon his face and laughed. And he said in his heart,

> "Can a child be born to a man a hundred years old, or can Sa-rah bear a child at ninety?"

(18) And Av-ra-ham said to הָאֱלֹהִים (the Elohim),

> "Oh that Yish-ma-el might live before You!"

(19) וַיֹּאמֶר אֱלֹהִים (And Elohim said)

אֲבָל שָׂרָה אִשְׁתְּךָ

יֹלֶדֶת לְךָ בֵּן

Nevertheless, Sa-rah your wife
shall bear a son for you,

וְקָרָאתָ אֶת-שְׁמוֹ יִצְחָק
וַהֲקִמֹתִי
אֶת-בְּרִיתִי אִתּוֹ
לִבְרִית עוֹלָם
לְזַרְעוֹ אַחֲרָיו

and you shall call * his name Isaac.
And I will set up
* My covenant with * him
for a covenant forever
for his seed after him.

(20)

וּלְיִשְׁמָעֵאל שְׁמַעְתִּיךָ
הִנֵּה בֵּרַכְתִּי אֹתוֹ
וְהִפְרֵיתִי אֹתוֹ
וְהִרְבֵּיתִי אֹתוֹ בִּמְאֹד מְאֹד
שְׁנֵים-עָשָׂר נְשִׂיאִם יוֹלִיד
וּנְתַתִּיו לְגוֹי גָּדוֹל

And to Ishmael, I have heard you.
Behold, I bless * him
and I make * him fruitful,
and I increase * him in much excess.
He shall beget twelve princes,
and I appoint him for a great nation.

Level One   בְּרֵאשִׁית ~ יז

(21)

וְאֶת־בְּרִיתִי

אָקִים אֶת־יִצְחָק

אֲשֶׁר תֵּלֵד לְךָ שָׂרָה

לַמּוֹעֵד הַזֶּה

בַּשָּׁנָה הָאַחֶרֶת

and * My covenant

I will set up with Isaac,

whom Sa-rah shall bear to you

for this appointed time

in the following year.

(22) וַיְכַל לְדַבֵּר (And He finished to speak) with אִתּוֹ (* him) וַיַּעַל אֱלֹהִים (Elohim ascended) from Av-ra-ham.

Abraham's Household Circumcised

(23) And Av-ra-ham took אֶת Yish-ma-el his son וְאֵת (and *) all who were born of his house וְאֵת (and *) all those acquired by his money, every male among the men of Av-ra-ham's house, and he circumcised אֶת the flesh of their foreskin on the same day that דִּבֶּר אִתּוֹ אֱלֹהִים (Elohim spoke with * him).

(24) Av-ra-ham was ninety-nine years old when he circumcised the flesh of his foreskin.

(25) And Yish-ma-el his son was thirteen years old when he circumcised אֵת the flesh of his foreskin.

(26) Av-ra-ham and his son Yish-ma-el were circumcised on the same day.

(27) And all the men of his house, those born in the house, and those acquired by money מֵאֵת (*from* *) a son of a foreigner, were circumcised with אִתּוֹ (* *him*).

Chapter 18

YHVH Visits Abraham

(1) וַיֵּרָא יהוה (*And YHVH appeared*) to him by the oaks of Mam-re. And he was sitting in the doorway of the tent at the heat of the day.

(2) And he lifted up his eyes and saw, and behold, three men were standing near him. And he saw them and ran from the doorway of the tent to meet them. And he bowed down to the ground.

(3) And he said,

> אֲדֹנָי (*My Lord*), if I have found favor in Your eyes do not pass by Your servant."

(4)

> "Let a little water be brought and wash Your feet, and rest under the tree."

(5)

> "And let me bring a piece of bread, then refresh Yourselves. Afterward You can pass by, because this is why You have come to Your servant."

And they said

> "Yes, do as you have said."

(6) Then Av-ra-ham hastened into the tent to Sa-rah, and he said,

> "Quickly -- make three seahs of fine flour for kneading and make bread cakes!"

Genesis ~ 18

(7) And Av-ra-ham ran to the herd and took a calf, tender and good, and gave it to the young man, and he made haste to prepare אֹתוֹ (* him).

(8) Then he took curds and milk, and the calf which he prepared, and set it before them. And he was standing by them under the tree while they ate.

(9) And they said to him,

> Where is Sarah your wife?

And he said,

> "Here, in the tent."

Isaac's Birth Foretold Again

(10) וַיֹּאמֶר (And He said),

> שׁוֹב אָשׁוּב אֵלֶיךָ
>
> כָּעֵת חַיָּה
>
> וְהִנֵּה־בֵן לְשָׂרָה אִשְׁתֶּךָ
>
> *I will certainly return to you*
>
> *like the season of living,*
>
> *and behold, a son to Sa-rah your wife.*

Now Sa-rah was listening at the doorway of the tent, and which was behind him.

(11) Now Av-ra-ham and Sa-rah were old, advanced in age; the way of women had ceased to be for Sa-rah.

(12) So Sa-rah laughed to herself saying,

> "After I am worn out וַאדֹנִי (and my lord) is old, shall this pleasure be to me?"

Level One   בְּרֵאשִׁית ~ יח

(13) וַיֹּאמֶר יהוה (*YHVH said*) to Av-ra-ham,

> לָמָּה זֶּה צָחֲקָה שָׂרָה לֵאמֹר
>
> הַאַף אֻמְנָם אֵלֵד
>
> וַאֲנִי זָקַנְתִּי

What is this that Sa-rah laughed, saying,

Indeed, truly I shall give birth,

and I am old?

(14)

> הֲיִפָּלֵא מֵיהוה דָּבָר
>
> לַמּוֹעֵד אָשׁוּב אֵלֶיךָ
>
> כָּעֵת חַיָּה
>
> וּלְשָׂרָה בֵן

The thing shall be marvelous from YHVH.

I will return to you for the appointed time

like the season of living

and for Sa-rah - a son.

(15) But Sa-rah denied it, saying,

> "*I did not laugh,*"

because she was afraid.

    וַיֹּאמֶר (*He said*)

> לֹא כִּי צָחָקְתְּ

No, because you laughed.

Genesis ~ 18

(16) Then the men set out from there, and they looked down upon S'dom. And Av-ra-ham went with them to send them on their way.

Judgment Proclaimed Against Sodom and Gomorrah

(17) וַיהוה אָמָר *(And YHVH said)*

הַמְכַסֶּה אֲנִי מֵאַבְרָהָם
אֲשֶׁר אֲנִי עֹשֶׂה

*Shall I conceal from Abraham
what I am doing?*

(18)

וְאַבְרָהָם הָיוֹ יִהְיֶה
לְגוֹי גָּדוֹל וְעָצוּם
וְנִבְרְכוּ-בוֹ
כֹּל גּוֹיֵי הָאָרֶץ

*Abraham will surely be
for a great and strong nation,
and they shall be blessed in him -
and all the nations of the land.*

(19)

כִּי יְדַעְתִּיו לְמַעַן אֲשֶׁר
יְצַוֶּה אֶת-בָּנָיו
וְאֶת-בֵּיתוֹ אַחֲרָיו
וְשָׁמְרוּ דֶּרֶךְ יהוה

Level One

בְּרֵאשִׁית ~ יח

Because I know him for the purpose that

*he will command * his sons*

*and * his house after him*

and they will keep the way of YHVH

לַעֲשׂוֹת צְדָקָה וּמִשְׁפָּט

לְמַעַן הָבִיא יהוה

עַל־אַבְרָהָם

אֵת אֲשֶׁר־דִּבֶּר עָלָיו

to do righteousness and justice,

for the purpose YHVH may bring

on Av-ra-ham

* what He said on him.

(20) וַיֹּאמֶר יהוה (*And YHVH said*)

זַעֲקַת סְדֹם וַעֲמֹרָה

כִּי־רָבָּה

וְחַטָּאתָם כִּי כָבְדָה מְאֹד

The outcry of Sodom and Gomorrah,

because it is much,

and their sin, because it is very grievous,

(21)

אֵרֲדָה־נָּא וְאֶרְאֶה

I will go down now and I will see.

Genesis ~ 18

הַכְּצַעֲקָתָהּ הַבָּאָה אֵלַי עָשׂוּ כָּלָה
וְאִם־לֹא אֵדָעָה

Have they done all of the cry that has come to Me?
And if not, I will know.

(22) And the men turned from there and went toward S'dom. And Av-ra-ham was still standing before יהוה (YHVH).

Abraham Bargains

(23) And Av-ra-ham drew near and said,

> "Will You also sweep away the righteous with the wicked?"

(24)

> "If perhaps there are fifty righteous in the midst of the city, will You also sweep them away and not forgive the place on account of the fifty righteous in her midst?"

(25)

> "Far be it from You to do such a thing as this, to kill the righteous with the wicked, that the righteous would be as the wicked! Far be it from You! Will not הֲשֹׁפֵט כָּל־הָאָרֶץ (the Judge of all the land) do justice?"

(26) וַיֹּאמֶר יהוה (And YHVH said)

אִם־אֶמְצָא בִסְדֹם
חֲמִשִּׁים צַדִּיקִם

Level One   בְּרֵאשִׁית ~ יח

If I find in Sodom
fifty righteous ones

בְּתוֹךְ הָעִיר
וְנָשָׂאתִי לְכָל־הַמָּקוֹם
בַּעֲבוּרָם

in the midst of the city,
then I will bear for the whole place
on account of them.

(27) Then Av-ra-ham answered and said,

"Look, please, I was bold to speak to אֲדֹנָי (my Lord) but I am dust and ashes."

(28)

"Perhaps the fifty righteous are lacking five. Will You destroy אֶת the whole city on account of the five?"

וַיֹּאמֶר (And He said)

לֹא אַשְׁחִית אִם־אֶמְצָא
שָׁם אַרְבָּעִים וַחֲמִשָּׁה

I will not destroy it if I find
there forty-five.

(29) And once again he spoke to Him and said,

"What if forty are found there?"

Genesis ~ 18

וַיֹּ֙אמֶר֙ (And He said)

> לֹ֣א אֶֽעֱשֶׂ֔ה
>
> בַּעֲב֖וּר הָאַרְבָּעִֽים
>
> *I will not do it*
>
> *on account of the forty.*

(30) And he said,

> "Please לַֽאדֹנָי֙ (for my Lord) must not be angry, and I will speak. What if thirty be found there?"

וַיֹּ֙אמֶר֙ (And He said)

> לֹ֣א אֶֽעֱשֶׂ֔ה אִם־אֶמְצָ֥א
>
> שָׁ֖ם שְׁלֹשִֽׁים
>
> *I will not do it if I find*
>
> *there thirty.*

(31) And he said,

> "Please, now, I was bold to speak to אֲדֹנָ֔י (my Lord) What if twenty be found there?"

וַיֹּ֙אמֶר֙ (And He said)

> לֹ֣א אַשְׁחִ֔ית
>
> בַּעֲב֖וּר הָעֶשְׂרִֽים
>
> *I will not destroy it*
>
> *on account of the twenty.*

Level One   בְּרֵאשִׁית ~ יח

(32) And he said,

"Please לַאדֹנָי (for my Lord) must not be angry, and I will speak only once more. What if ten are found there?"

וַיֹּאמֶר (And He said)

לֹא אַשְׁחִית

בַּעֲבוּר הָעֲשָׂרָה

I will not destroy it

on account of the ten.

(33) וַיֵּלֶךְ יהוה (And YHVH went) as He finished speaking to Av-ra-ham, and Av-ra-ham returned to his place.

Chapter 19

Saving Lot

(1) And two of הַמַּלְאָכִים (*the messengers*) came to S'dom in the evening. And Lot was sitting in the gateway of S'dom. Then Lot saw them and stood up to meet them. And he bowed down with his face to the ground.

(2) And he said,

> "Behold אֲדֹנַי (*my lords*), please turn aside into the house of your servant and spend the night and wash your feet. Then you can rise early and go on your way."

And they said,

> "No, because we will lodge in the square."

(3) But he urged them strongly, and they turned aside with him and came into his house. And he made a meal for them and baked unleavened bread, and they ate.

(4) Before they laid down, the men of the city, the men of S'dom surrounded the house, from the young man and unto old, all the people from the outskirts.

(5) And they called to Lot and said to him,

> "Where are the men who came to you tonight? Bring them out to us so that we may know אֹתָם (** them*)."

(6) But Lot went out to them at the entrance, and he shut the door behind him.

(7) And he said,

> "It must not be, please, my brothers, you are doing evil."

Level One   בְּרֵאשִׁית ~ יט

(8)

> "Behold, please, I have two daughters who have not known a man. Please, let me bring אֶתְהֶן (* them) out to you; then do to them כַּטּוֹב (as the good) in your eyes. Only to these men do not do this thing, since they came under my roof for protection."

(9) But they said,

> "Step aside!"

Then they said,

> "This fellow came to dwell as a foreigner and he acts as a judge! Now we shall do worse to you than them!"

And they pressed very hard against the man, against Lot, and they drew near to break the door.

(10) Then the men reached out with אֶת their hands and brought אֶת Lot in to them into the house they shut וְאֶת (and *) the door.

(11) וְאֶת (and *) the men who were at the entrance of the house they struck with blindness, both small and great, and they were unable to find the entrance.

(12) And the men said to Lot,

> "Who here is still for you? Son-in-law, and your sons, and your daughters, and all who are for you in the city, bring them forth from this place.

(13)

> "Because we are about to destroy אֶת this place, because their cry has become great in אֶת the face of יהוה (YHVH) and וַיְשַׁלְּחֵנוּ יהוה (YHVH sent us) to destroy it."

(14) Then Lot went out and spoke to his sons-in-law who married his daughters and said,

> "Get up! Go out from this place, because יהוה (YHVH) is going to destroy אֶת the city!"

But it seemed like a joke in the eyes of his sons-in-law.

(15) And as the dawn came up הַמַּלְאָכִים (*the messengers*) urged Lot saying,

> "Get up, take אֶת your wife and וְאֶת two of your daughters found here, lest you be destroyed in the punishment of the city."

(16) But when he lingered, the men seized him by his hand and his wife's hand, and his two daughters by hand, on account of the mercy of יהוה (YHVH) upon him. And they brought him out and set him outside of the city.

(17) And after bringing אֹתָם (** them*) outside one said,

> "Escape on account of your soul; do not look behind you, and do not stand in all the plain. Escape toward the mountains lest you be destroyed."

(18) And Lot said to them,

> "No, please אֲדֹנָי (*my lord*)."

(19)

> "Behold, your servant has found favor in your eyes and you have shown me great kindness in saving אֶת my life. But I cannot flee to the mountains, lest הָרָעָה (*the evil*) overtakes me and I die.

(20)

> "Behold, this city is near enough to flee there, and it is a little one.

Level One בְּרֵאשִׁית ~ יט

> *Please, let me flee there. Is it not a little one? Then my life shall be saved."*

(21) And he said to him,

> *"Behold, I will lift up your faces also to this thing; that I will not overthrow * the city of which you speak."*

(22)

> *"Escape there quickly, because I am not able to do a thing until you get there."*

Therefore, there name of the city was called Zo-ar.

The Destruction Of Sodom And Gomorrah

(23) After the sun had risen upon the land and Lot had entered Zo-ar.

(24) וַיהוה הִמְטִיר (*And YHVH rained*) upon S'dom and A-mo-rah (Gomorrah) brimstone and fire מֵאֵת יהוה (*from * YHVH*) from the sky.

(25) וַיַּהֲפֹךְ (*And He overthrew*) אֶת the cities וְאֵת (*and **) and all the plain וְאֵת (*and **) all the inhabitants of the cities and the vegetation of the ground.

(26) But his wife looked back, and she became נְצִיב מֶלַח (*a monument of salt*).

(27) And Av-ra-ham arose early in the morning and went to the place he had stood there with אֶת the face of יהוה (*YHVH*).

(28) And he looked down upon the surface of S'dom and A-mo-rah (Gomorrah), and upon the whole surface of the land, the plain. And he saw that, behold, the smoke of the land went up like the smoke of a smelting furnace.

(29) So it was, when אֱלֹהִים (*Elohim*) destroyed אֶת the cities of the plain that וַיִּזְכֹּר אֱלֹהִים (*Elohim remembered*) אֶת Av-ra-ham וַיְשַׁלַּח (*and He sent*) אֶת Lot

109

out from the midst of the overthrow, when He overthrew את the cities in which Lot lived.

Birth Of The Moabites And The Ammonites

(30) And Lot went out from Zo-ar and settled in the hill country with his two daughters, for he was afraid to stay in Zo-ar.
So he lived in a cave, he and his two daughters.

(31) And the firstborn daughter said to the younger one,

> "Our father is old, and there is no man in the land to come in to us according to the manner of all the land."

(32)

> "Come, let us give את our father wine to drink and let us lie with him that we may keep alive seed from our father."

(33) And they gave את their father wine to drink that night, and the firstborn went and lay with את her father, but he did not know when she lay down or when she got up.

(34) And it happened that, the next day the firstborn said to the younger one,

> "Look, I laid with את my father last night. Let us give him wine to drink also tonight, then go and lie with him that we may keep alive seed from our father."

(35) And they gave את their father wine to drink again that night, and the younger got up and lay with him, but he did not know when she lay down or when she got up.

(36) And the two daughters of Lot became pregnant by their father.

Level One   בְּרֵאשִׁית ~ יט

(37) The firstborn gave birth to a son, and she called his name Mo-av. He is the father of Mo-av until this day.

(38) And the younger, she also gave birth to a son, and she called his name Ben-Am-mi. He is the father of the sons of Am-mon until this day.

Chapter 20

Abimelech Takes Sarah

(1) And Av-ra-ham journeyed from there to the land of the Ne-gev, and he settled between Ka-desh and Shur. And he sojourned in G'rar.

(2) And Av-ra-ham said about Sa-rah his wife,

> *"She is my sister."*

And A-vi-me-lech king of G'rar sent and took אֶת Sa-rah.

(3) וַיָּבֹא אֱלֹהִים (*And Elohim came*) to A-vi-me-lech in a dream at night וַיֹּאמֶר (*and He said*) to him,

> הִנְּךָ מֵת
> עַל-הָאִשָּׁה אֲשֶׁר-לָקַחְתָּ
> וְהִוא בְּעֻלַת בָּעַל
>
> *Behold, you are dying*
> *on account of the woman whom you took.*
> *And she in possession of a possessor.*

(4) Now A-vi-me-lech had not come near her, so he said,

> אֲדֹנָי (*My Lord*), will You even kill a righteous people?"

(5)

> *"Did not he himself say to me,*
>
> *'She is my sister?' "*
>
> *"And she herself said,*

Level One   בְּרֵאשִׁית ~ כ

'He is my brother.'"

"With integrity of my heart and with cleanness of my hands I did this."

(6) וַיֹּאמֶר הָאֱלֹהִים (*And the Elohim*) said to him in the dream,

גַּם אָנֹכִי יָדַעְתִּי כִּי
בְתָם־לְבָבְךָ עָשִׂיתָ זֹּאת
וָאֶחְשֹׂךְ גַּם־אָנֹכִי אוֹתְךָ מֵחֲטוֹ־לִי
עַל־כֵּן לֹא־נְתַתִּיךָ לִנְגֹּעַ אֵלֶיהָ

I also know that
in the integrity of your heart you did this,
and I also kept * you from sinning to Me.
Therefore, I did not allow you to touch her.

(7)

וְעַתָּה הָשֵׁב אֵשֶׁת־הָאִישׁ
כִּי־נָבִיא הוּא
וְיִתְפַּלֵּל בַּעַדְךָ וֶחְיֵה
וְאִם־אֵינְךָ מֵשִׁיב

And now, restore the wife of the man,
because he is a prophet,
and he will pray for you and you will live.
And if you do not restore,

Genesis ~ 20

דַּע כִּי־מוֹת תָּמוּת
אַתָּה וְכָל־אֲשֶׁר־לָךְ

know that you will surely die,
you and all that are for you.

(8) So A-vi-me-lech rose early in the morning. And he called all his servants and told them אֵת all these words in their ears, and the men were very afraid.

(9) And A-vi-me-lech called for Av-ra-ham and said to him,

> "What have you done to us? And how have I sinned against you that you brought upon me and upon my kingdom a great sin? You have done things to me that should not be done."

(10) And A-vi-me-lech said to Av-ra-ham,

> "What did you see that you did אֵת this thing?"

(11) And Av-ra-ham said,

> "Because I thought, surely there is no fear of אֱלֹהִים (Elohim) in this place; they will kill me on account of my wife."

(12)

> "And also, truly she is my sister, the daughter of my father, but not the daughter of my mother. And she became my wife."

(13)

> "And it happened that as אֱלֹהִים (Elohim) caused אֹתִי (* me) to wander from the house of my father I said to her,
>
>> 'This is your loyal kindness that you must do for me at every

place where we come: say concerning me,

"He is my brother.' "

Sarah Is Returned To Abraham

(14) And A-vi-me-lech took sheep and cattle and male servants and female servants, and he gave them to Av-ra-ham. And he returned אֵת Sa-rah his wife to him.

(15) And A-vi-me-lech said,

"Here is my land before you; בַּטּוֹב (in the good) in your eyes, settle."

(16) And to Sa-rah he said,

"Look, I have given a thousand pieces of silver to your brother. Behold, it shall be for you a covering of eyes. For all who are with אִתָּךְ (you) וְאֵת (and *) by all this she was corrected."*

(17) And Av-ra-ham prayed to הָאֱלֹהִים (the Elohim) and וַיִּרְפָּא אֱלֹהִים (Elohim healed) אֵת A-vi-me-lech וְאֵת (and *) his wife and his female servants so that they could bear children again.

(18) כִּי-עָצֹר עָצַר יהוה (For YHVH surely restrained) all the wombs of the house of A-vi-me-lech because of the matter of Sa-rah, the wife of Av-ra-ham.

Chapter 21

Birth Of Isaac

(1) וַיְהוָה פָּקַד (And YHVH visited) אֶת Sa-rah as אָמַר (He had said) וַיַּעַשׂ יהוה (and YHVH did) to Sa-rah as דִּבֶּר (He had spoken).

(2) And she conceived, and Sa-rah bore to Av-ra-ham a son in his old age at the appointed time that דִּבֶּר אֹתוֹ אֱלֹהִים (Elohim had told* him).

(3) And Av-ra-ham called אֶת the name of his son who was born to him, whom Sa-rah bore to him, Yitz-khak (*Isaac*).

(4) And Av-ra-ham circumcised אֶת Yitz-khak (*Isaac*) his son when he was eight days old, as צִוָּה אֹתוֹ אֱלֹהִים (Elohim had instructed * him).

(5) And Av-ra-ham was a hundred years old when אֶת Yitz-khak (*Isaac*) his son was born to him.

(6) And Sa-rah said,

> עָשָׂה אֱלֹהִים (Elohim has made) laughter for me; all who hear will laugh for me."

(7) And she said,

> "Who would announce to Av-ra-ham that Sa-rah would nurse children? Yet I have borne a son to Av-ra-ham in his old age."

Hagar and Ishmael Sent Away

(8) And the child grew and was weaned. And Av-ra-ham made a great feast on the day אֶת Yitz-khak (*Isaac*) was weaned.

Level One   בְּרֵאשִׁית ~ כא

(9) And Sa-rah saw אֵת the son of Ha-gar the Mitz-rit (*Egyptian*), whom she had borne Av-ra-ham, mocking.

(10) Then she said to Av-ra-ham,

> "Drive out this slave woman וְאֶת (and *) her son, for the son of this slave woman will not be heir with my son, with Yitz-khak (*Isaac*)."

(11) And the word was exceedingly evil in the eyes of Av-ra-ham on account of his son.

(12) וַיֹּאמֶר אֱלֹהִים (*And Elohim said*) to Av-ra-ham,

אַל־יֵרַע בְּעֵינֶיךָ

עַל־הַנַּעַר וְעַל־אֲמָתֶךָ

כֹּל אֲשֶׁר תֹּאמַר אֵלֶיךָ שָׂרָה

שְׁמַע בְּקֹלָהּ

כִּי בְיִצְחָק יִקָּרֵא לְךָ זָרַע

> *It must not be evil in your eyes*
> *on account of the young man and your maidservant.*
> *All that Sarah is saying to you,*
> *hear in her voice,*
> *because in Isaac your seed will be called.*

(13)

וְגַם אֶת־בֶּן־הָאָמָה

*And also * the son of the maidservant,*

לְגוֹי אֲשִׂימֶנּוּ

כִּי זַרְעֲךָ הוּא

for a nation, I will appoint him,
because he is your seed.

(14) Then Av-ra-ham rose up early in the morning and took bread and a skin of water and gave it to Ha-gar, putting it on her shoulder וְאֶת (*and **) the boy, and he sent her away and she went, wandering about in the wilderness of Ber~Sha-va.

Elohim Hears Ishmael

(15) And when the water was finished from the skin, she put אֶת the boy under one of the bushes.

(16) And she went and she sat a good distance away, for she said,

"Let me not see the death of the boy."

So she sat away from him and lifted up אֶת her voice and wept.

(17) וַיִּשְׁמַע אֱלֹהִים (*And Elohim heard*) אֶת the voice of the young man וַיִּקְרָא מַלְאַךְ אֱלֹהִים (*and the messenger of Elohim called*) to Ha-gar from the sky and said to her,

מַה־לָּךְ הָגָר

אַל־תִּירְאִי

כִּי־שָׁמַע אֱלֹהִים

אֶל־קוֹל הַנַּעַר

בַּאֲשֶׁר הוּא־שָׁם

Level One   בְּרֵאשִׁית ~ כא

What is to you Hagar?
You must not fear,
because Elohim has listened
to the voice of the young man
in that he is there.

(18)

קוּמִי שְׂאִי אֶת־הַנַּעַר
וְהַחֲזִיקִי אֶת־יָדֵךְ בּוֹ
כִּי־לְגוֹי גָּדוֹל
אֲשִׂימֶנּוּ

Get up, lift up * the young man
and grip on him with * your hand,
because for a great nation
I will appoint him.

(19) וַיִּפְקַח אֱלֹהִים (*And Elohim opened*) אֶת her eyes, and she saw a well of water. And she went and filled אֶת the flask with water and gave a drink to אֶת the young man.

(20) וַיְהִי אֱלֹהִים (*And Elohim was*) with אֶת the young man, and he grew and lived in the wilderness. And he became an expert with a bow.

(21) And he lived in the wilderness of Pa-ran. And his mother took a wife for him from the land of Mitz-ra-yim (*Egypt*).

Genesis ~ 21

Abraham Covenants With Abimelech

(22) And it happened that at that time, A-vi-me-lech and Fi-khol, the commander of his army, said to Av-ra-ham,

> אֱלֹהִים (Elohim) is with you, in all that אַתָּה (you) do."

(23)

> "So now, swear to me here בֵּאלֹהִים (on Elohim) that you will not deal with me falsely, or with my descendants, or my posterity. According to the kindness that I have done to you, you shall pledge to do with me and with the land where you sojourn in."

(24) And Av-ra-ham said,

> "I swear."

(25) Then Av-ra-ham corrected אֶת A-vi-me-lech on account of the well of water that servants of A-vi-me-lech had seized.

(26) And A-vi-me-lech said,

> "I do not know who did אֶת this thing, and also אַתָּה (you) did not tell me, nor have I heard of it except for today."

(27) And Av-ra-ham took sheep and cattle and gave them to A-vi-me-lech. And the two of them made a covenant.

(28) Then Av-ra-ham set off אֶת seven ewe lambs of the flock by themselves.

(29) And A-vi-me-lech said to Av-ra-ham,

> "What is the meaning of these seven ewe lambs that you have set off by themselves?"

Level One   בְּרֵאשִׁית ~ כא

(30) And he said,

> "You shall take אֶת seven ewe lambs from my hand as proof on my behalf that I dug אֶת this well."

(31) Therefore, that place is called בְּאֵר שָׁבַע (*Beer-Sheba*), because there the two of them נִשְׁבְּעוּ (*they swore*).

(32) And they made a covenant at Ber~Sha-va. And A-vi-me-lech, and Fi-khol his army commander stood and returned to the land of the P'lish-tim (*Philistines*).

(33) And he planted a tamarisk tree in Ber~Sha-va, and there he called on the name of יהוה אֵל עוֹלָם (*YHVH, El Everlasting*).

(34) And Av-ra-ham sojourned in the land of the P'lish-tim (*Philistines*) many days.

Chapter 22

Sacrificing Isaac

(1) And it happened that after these things וְהָאֱלֹהִים נִסָּה (*and the Elohim tested*) אֶת Av-ra-ham וַיֹּאמֶר (*and He said*) to him,

אַבְרָהָם

Abraham

And he said,

"Here I am."

(2) וַיֹּאמֶר (*and He said*)

קַח־נָא אֶת־בִּנְךָ
אֶת־יְחִידְךָ
אֲשֶׁר־אָהַבְתָּ אֶת־יִצְחָק
וְלֶךְ־לְךָ אֶל־אֶרֶץ הַמֹּרִיָּה

*Please take * your son,*
* your only one
*whom you love, * Isaac,*
and go for yourself to the land of the Moriah,

וְהַעֲלֵהוּ שָׁם לְעֹלָה
עַל אַחַד הֶהָרִים
אֲשֶׁר אֹמַר אֵלֶיךָ

Level One   בְּרֵאשִׁית ~ כב

> *and offer him there for a burnt offering*
> *on one of the mountains*
> *where I will tell you.*

(3) And Av-ra-ham rose up early in the morning and saddled אֶת his donkey. And he took אֵת two of his young men with אִתּוֹ (* *him*) וְאֵת (*and* *) Yitz-khak (*Isaac*) his son. And he chopped wood for a burnt offering. And he got up and went to the place which אָמַר הָאֱלֹהִים (*the Elohim had told*) to him.

(4) On the third day Av-ra-ham lifted up אֶת his eyes, and he saw אֶת the place at a distance.

(5) And Av-ra-ham said to his young men,

> *"You stay here with the donkey, and I and the young man will go up there. We will worship, then we will return to you."*

(6) And Av-ra-ham took אֶת the wood of the burnt offering and placed it on Yitz-khak (*Isaac*) his son. And he took אֶת the fire in his hand וְאֶת (*and* *) the knife, and the two of them went together.

(7) And Yitz-khak (*Isaac*) said to Av-ra-ham his father,

> *"My father."*

And he said,

> *"Here I am, my son."*

And he said,

> *"Here is the fire and the wood, but where is the lamb for a burnt offering?"*

(8) And Av-ra-ham said,

Genesis ~ 22

אֱלֹהִים יִרְאֶה (*Elohim shall see*) *for Himself the lamb for a burnt offering, my son."*

And the two of them went together.

(9) And they came to the place that אָמַר הָאֱלֹהִים (*the Elohim said*) to him. And Av-ra-ham built אֶת the altar there and arranged אֶת the wood. Then he bound אֶת Yitz-khak (*Isaac*) his son and placed אֹתוֹ (* *him*) on the altar atop the wood.

(10) And Av-ra-ham stretched out אֶת his hand and took אֶת the knife to slaughter אֶת his son.

(11) וַיִּקְרָא מַלְאַךְ יהוה (*And the messenger of YHVH called*) to him from the sky וַיֹּאמֶר (*and He said*)

אַבְרָהָם אַבְרָהָם

Abraham Abraham

And he said,

"Here I am."

(12) וַיֹּאמֶר (*and He said*)

אַל־תִּשְׁלַח יָדְךָ

אֶל־הַנַּעַר

וְאַל־תַּעַשׂ לוֹ מְאוּמָה

כִּי עַתָּה יָדַעְתִּי

You must not stretch your hand

to the young man;

and you must not do anything to him,

because now I know

Level One   בְּרֵאשִׁית ~ כב

כִּי־יְרֵא אֱלֹהִים אַתָּה
וְלֹא חָשַׂכְתָּ אֶת־בִּנְךָ
אֶת־יְחִידְךָ מִמֶּנִּי

that you are fearing of Elohim
*and you have not kept back * your son,*
** your only one, from Me.*

(13) And Av-ra-ham lifted up אֶת his eyes and looked. And behold, a ram was caught in the thicket by his horns. And Av-ra-ham went and took אֶת the ram, and offered it as a burnt offering in place of his son.

(14) And Av-ra-ham called the name of that place יהוה יִרְאֶה (YHVH, He will see) for which reason it is said today,

"On the mountain יהוה יֵרָאֶה (YHVH, He will see)."

(15) וַיִּקְרָא מַלְאַךְ יהוה (And the messenger of YHVH called) to Av-ra-ham a second time from the sky.

(16) וַיֹּאמֶר (and He said)

בִּי נִשְׁבַּעְתִּי נְאֻם־יהוה
כִּי יַעַן אֲשֶׁר עָשִׂיתָ אֶת־הַדָּבָר הַזֶּה
וְלֹא חָשַׂכְתָּ אֶת־בִּנְךָ אֶת־יְחִידֶךָ

On Myself I swear, declares YHVH,
*that inasmuch that you have done * this thing*
*and have not kept back * your son, * your only one.*

Genesis ~ 22

(17)

כִּי־בָרֵךְ אֲבָרֶכְךָ

וְהַרְבָּה אַרְבֶּה אֶת־זַרְעֲךָ

כְּכוֹכְבֵי הַשָּׁמַיִם

וְכַחוֹל אֲשֶׁר עַל־שְׂפַת הַיָּם

וְיִרַשׁ זַרְעֲךָ

אֵת שַׁעַר אֹיְבָיו

That I will certainly bless you
and the increase of * your seed I shall increase
like the stars of the sky,
and as the sand that is on the shore of the sea.
And your seed will overtake
* the gate of his enemies.

(18)

וְהִתְבָּרְכוּ בְזַרְעֲךָ

כֹּל גּוֹיֵי הָאָרֶץ

עֵקֶב אֲשֶׁר שָׁמַעְתָּ בְּקֹלִי

And they bless themselves in your seed –
all the nations of the land,
inasmuch that you have heard in My voice.

(19) And Av~ra~ham returned to his servants, and they got up and went together to Ber~Sha~va. And Av~ra~ham lived in Ber~Sha~va.

Level One

בְּרֵאשִׁית ~ כב

Descendants Of Nakhor

(20) And it happened that after these things, it was told to Av-ra-ham,

"Look, Mil-kah has also borne children to your brother Na-khor.

(21-22)

אֶת Utz his firstborn וְאֶת (and *) Buz his brother וְאֶת (and *) K'mu-el the father of A-ram. וְאֶת (and *) Ke-sed וְאֶת (and *) Kha-zo וְאֶת (and *) Pil-dash וְאֶת (and *) Yid-laf וְאֶת (and *) B'tu-el."

(23)

"And B'tu-el fathered אֵת Riv-kah (Rebekah). These eight Mil-kah bore to Na-khor, the brother of Av-ra-ham."

(24)

"And his concubine, whose name was R'u-mah, also bore אֶת Te-vakh וְאֶת (and *) Ga-kham וְאֶת (and *) Ta-khash וְאֶת (and *) Ma-a-khah."

Chapter 23

Death Of Sarah

(1) And Sa-rah lived one hundred and twenty-seven years; these were the years of the life of Sa-rah.

(2) And Sa-rah died in Kir-yat~Ar-ba; that is Hev-ron, in the land of K'na-an.

Abraham's Burial Spot

(3) And Av-ra-ham went to mourn for Sa-rah and to weep for her. And Av-ra-ham rose up from his dead, and he spoke to the sons of Khet and said,

(4)

> *"I am a sojourner and a guest among you; give to me my own burial site among you so that I may bury my dead from before me."*

(5) And the sons of Khet answered אֶת Av-ra-ham and said to him,

(6)

> *"Hear us* אֲדֹנִי *(my lord)* אַתָּה *(you) are a prince of* אֱלֹהִים *(Elohim) in our midst. Bury* אֶת *your dead in the choicest of our burial sites. None of us will withhold* אֶת *his burial site from you for burying your dead."*

(7) And Av-ra-ham rose up and bowed to the people of the land, to the sons of Khet.

(8) And he spoke with אִתָּם (* them), saying,

> *"If it is with* אֶת *your soul that I bury* אֶת *my dead from before me,*

Level One

בְּרֵאשִׁית ~ כג

> *hear me and intercede for me with Ef-ron the son of Tzo-khar."*

(9)
> *"And may he sell to me* אֶת *the cave of Makh-pe-lah which belongs to him, which is at the end of his field. Let him sell it to me at full value in your midst as a burial site."*

(10) Now Ef-ron was sitting among the sons of Khet. And Ef-ron the Khit-ti (*Hittite*) answered אֶת Av-ra-ham in the hearing of the sons of Khet with respect to all who were entering the gate of his city, and said,

(11)
> *"No* אֲדֹנִי *(my lord), hear me. I give you the field and the cave which is in it, I also give it to you in the sight of the children of my people I give it to you. Bury your dead."*

(12) And Av-ra-ham bowed before the people of the land.

(13) And he spoke to Ef-ron in the hearing of the people of the land, saying,

> *"Yea, O that if* אַתָּה *(you) will hear me -- I give the price of the field. Take it from me that I may bury* אֶת *my dead there."*

(14) And Ef-ron answered אֶת Av-ra-ham, saying to him,

(15)
> אֲדֹנִי *(My lord), hear me. A piece of land worth four hundred shekels of silver -- what is that between me and you?* וְאֶת *(and *) your dead - bury."*

(16) Then Av-ra-ham listened to Ef-ron, and Av-ra-ham weighed for Ef-ron אֶת the silver that he had named in the hearing of the sons of Khet: four hundred shekels of silver passing to the merchant.

Genesis ~ 23

(17) And it was confirmed that the field of Ef-ron in the Makh-pe-lah, which was near Mam-re -- the field and the cave which was in it, with all the trees that were in the field, which were in all its boundary around about --

(18) to Av-ra-ham as a property in the presence of the sons of Khet, with respect to all who were entering the gate of his city.

(19) So then afterward, Av-ra-ham buried אֶת Sa-rah his wife in the cave of the field of Makh-pe-lah near Mam-re; that is Hev-ron, in the land of K'na-an.

(20) And the field and the cave which was in it passed to Av-ra-ham as a burial site מֵאֵת (*from ＊*) the sons of Khet.

Chapter 24

Isaac's Bride

(1) And Av-ra-ham was old, advanced in age וַיהוה בֵּרַךְ (and YHVH had blessed) אֶת Av-ra-ham in everything.

(2) And Av-ra-ham said to his servant, the oldest of his house, who had charge of all he had,

> "Please put your hand under my thigh."

(3)

> "And I make you swore בַּיהוה אֱלֹהֵי הַשָּׁמַיִם (on YHVH, Elohim of the sky) וֵאלֹהֵי הָאָרֶץ (and Elohim of the land) that you will not take a wife for my son from the daughters of the K'na-a-ni (Canaanite) in whose midst I am dwelling."

(4)

> "That you will go to my land and to my family, and take a wife for my son, for Yitz-khak (Isaac)."

(5) And the servant said to him,

> "Perhaps the woman will not be willing to follow me to this land -- must I then return אֶת your son to the land from whence you came?"

(6) Av-ra-ham said to him,

> "You must take care that you do not bring אֶת my son there."

Genesis ~ 24

(7)

יהוה אֱלֹהֵי הַשָּׁמַיִם (YHVH, Elohim of the sky) Who took me from the house of my father and from the land of my family, and Who spoke to me and swore to me, saying,

לְזַרְעֲךָ אֶתֵּן

אֶת-הָאָרֶץ הַזֹּאת

To your seed I will give
* this land,

"He will send מַלְאָכוֹ (His messenger) before you, and you shall take a wife for my son from there."

(8)

"And if the woman is not willing to follow you, then you shall be released from this oath of mine -- but you must not bring אֶת my son there."

(9) Then the servant put אֶת his hand under the thigh of Av-ra-ham אֲדֹנָיו (his lord), and he swore to him concerning this matter.

(10) And the servant took ten camels from the camels of אֲדֹנָיו (his lord), and he went with all טוּב (good of) אֲדֹנָיו (his lord) in his hand. And he arose and went to A-ram~Na-ha-ra-yim, to the city of Na-khor.

(11) And he made the camels kneel outside the city at the well of water, at the time of evening, toward the time the women went out to draw water.

(12) And he said,

יהוה אֱלֹהֵי אֲדֹנִי אַבְרָהָם (YHVH, Elohim of my lord Av-ra-ham)

Level One   בְּרֵאשִׁית ~ כד

please grant me success today and show kindness to אֲדֹנִי *(my lord) Av-ra-ham."*

(13) *"Behold, I am standing by the spring of water, and the daughters of the men of the city are going out to draw water."*

(14) *"And let it be that the young woman to whom I shall say,*

     'Please, offer your jar that I may drink,'

and who says,

     'Drink -- and I will also water your camels,'

אֹתָהּ *(* her) You have chosen for Your servant, for Yitz-khak (Isaac). By her I will know that You have shown kindness to* אֲדֹנִי *(my lord)."*

Rebekah Waters The Camels

(15) And it happened that before he had finished speaking, behold, Riv-kah (Rebekah) -- who was born to B'tu-el, son of Mil-kah, the wife of Na-khor, the brother of Av-ra-ham -- came out, and her jar was on her shoulder.

(16) And the young woman was טֹבַת (*good of*) appearance. She was a virgin; no man had known her. And she went down to the spring, filled her jar, and came up.

(17) And the servant ran to meet her. And he said,

     "Please, let me drink a little of the water from your jar."

Genesis ~ 24

(18) And she said,

> "Drink אֲדֹנִי (my lord)."

And she quickly lowered her jar in her hand and gave him a drink.

(19) When she finished giving him a drink she said,

> "I will also draw water for your camels until they finish drinking."

(20) And she quickly emptied her jar into the trough and ran again to the well to draw water. And she drew water for all his camels.

(21) And the man was gazing at her silently to know if יהוה (YHVH) had made his journey successful or not.

(22) And it happened that as the camels finished drinking the man took a gold ring of a half shekel in weight and two bracelets for her arms, ten shekels in weight,

(23) and said,

> "Please tell me, whose daughter are אַתְּ (you)? Is there a place at the house of your father for us to spend the night?"

(24) And she said to him,

> "I am the daughter of B'tu-el, son of Mil-kah, whom she bore to Na-khor."

(25) Then she said to him,

> "We have both straw and fodder in abundance, as well as a place to spend the night."

(26) And the man knelt down and he worshiped לַיהוה (to YHVH).

(27) And he said,

"Blessed be יהוה אֱלֹהֵי אֲדֹנִי אַבְרָהָם (YHVH, Elohim of my lord Av-ra-ham), Who has not withheld His kindness and His faithfulness from אֲדֹנִי (my lord). I was on the way and נָחַנִי יהוה (YHVH guided me) to the house of the brother of אֲדֹנִי (my lord)."

(28) Then the young woman ran and reported these things to the household of her mother.

Servant Speaks With Rebekah's Family

(29) Now Riv-kah (*Rebekah*) had a brother, and his name was La-van. And La-van ran out to the man, toward the spring.

(30) And when he saw אֶת the ring וְאֶת (*and **) the bracelets on the arms of his sister and heard אֵת the words of Riv-kah (*Rebekah*) his sister, who said,

"Thus the man spoke to me..."

He went to the man. And behold, he was standing with the camels at the spring.

(31) And he said,

"Come, O blessed one of יהוה (*YHVH*). Why do you stand outside? Now I have prepared the house and a place for the camels."

(32) And the man came to the house and unloaded the camels. And he gave straw and fodder to the camels, and water to wash his feet and the feet of the men who were with אִתּוֹ (** him*).

(33) And food was placed before him to eat. And he said,

"I will not eat until I have told my errand."

And he said,

> "Speak."

(34) And he said,

> "I am the servant of Av-ra-ham.

(35)

> וַיהוה בֵּרַךְ (And YHVH has blessed) אֶת אֲדֹנִי (* my lord) exceedingly, and he has become great. He has given to him sheep and cattle, silver and gold, male servants and female servants, and camels and donkeys."

(36)

> "And Sa-rah, the wife of אֲדֹנִי (my lord), has borne a son לַאדֹנִי (to my lord) after her old age. And he has given to him אֶת all that he has."

(37)

> "And אֲדֹנִי (my lord) made me swear, saying,
>
>> 'Do not take a wife for my son from the daughters of the K'na-a-ni (Canaanite) in whose land I am living.'

(38)

>> 'But you shall go to the house of my father, and to my family, and you shall take a wife for my son.'

(39)

> "And I said to אֲדֹנִי (my lord),
>
>> 'Perhaps the woman will not follow me.'"

Level One   בְּרֵאשִׁית ~ כד

(40)

"And he said to me,

יהוה (YHVH) before Whom I have walked, shall send מַלְאָכוֹ (His messenger) with אִתָּךְ (* you) and will make your journey successful. And you shall take a wife for my son from my family, and from the house of my father.'

(41)

'Then you shall be released from my oath, when you come to my family. And if they will not give a woman to you, then you will be released from my oath.' "

(42)

"And today I came to the spring, and I said,

יהוה אֱלֹהֵי אֲדֹנִי אַבְרָהָם (YHVH, Elohim of my lord Av-ra-ham), if You would please make my journey successful, upon which I am going.'

(43)

'Behold, I am standing by the spring of water. Let it be that the young woman who comes out to draw water and to whom I say,

"Please give me a little water to drink from your jar."

(44)

'Let her say to me also,

אַתָּה (You) drink; I will also draw water for your camels."

Genesis ~ 24

'She is the wife that הֹכִיחַ יהוה (YHVH finds correct) for the son of אֲדֹנִי (my lord).' "

(45)

"I had not yet finished speaking to myself when, behold, Riv-kah (Rebekah) was coming out with her jar on her shoulder. And she went down to the spring and drew water. And I said to her,

'Please give me a drink.' "

(46)

"And she hastened and let down her jar from her shoulder and said,

'Drink, and I will give a drink to your camels also.' "

"And I drank and she gave a drink to the camels also."

(47)

"And I asked אֹתָהּ (* her) and said,

'Whose daughter are אַתְּ (you)?' "

"And she said,

'The daughter of B'tu-el, son of Na-khor, whom Mil-kah bore to him.' "

"And I put the ring on her nose and the bracelets on her arms."

(48)

"And I knelt down and I worshiped לַיהוה (to YHVH) and I blessed אֶת-יהוה אֱלֹהֵי אֲדֹנִי אַבְרָהָם (* YHVH, Elohim of my lord Av-ra-ham), Who led me on the right way, to take אֶת the daughter of the brother of אֲדֹנִי (my lord) for his son."

Level One   בְּרֵאשִׁית ~ כד

(49)

"So now, if you are going to deal kindly and truly with אֶת־אֲדֹנִי (* my lord), tell me. And if not, tell me, so that I may turn to the right or to the left."

(50) Then La-van and B'tu-el answered, and they said,

"The matter has gone out מֵיהוה (from YHVH) we are not able to speak רַע אוֹ־טוֹב (evil or good) to you."

(51)

"Here is Riv-kah (Rebekah) before you. Take her and go; let her be a wife for the son of אֲדֹנֶיךָ (your lord) as יהוה (YHVH) has spoken."

(52) And it happened that when the servant of Av-ra-ham heard אֵת their words he bowed down to the ground לַיהוה (to YHVH).

(53) And the servant brought out silver jewelry and gold jewelry, and garments, and he gave them to Riv-kah (Rebekah). And he gave precious gifts to her brother and to her mother.

Rebekah Leaves Her Family

(54) And he and the men who were with him ate and drank, and they spent the night. And they got up in the morning, and he said,

"Let me go לַאדֹנִי (to my lord)."

(55) And her brother and her mother said,

"Let the young woman remain with אִתָּנוּ (* us) ten days or so;

Genesis ~ 24

after that she may go."

(56) And he said to them,

"You must not delay אֹתִי (* me) וַיהוה (and YHVH) has made my journey successful. Let me go. I must go לַאדֹנִי (to my lord)."

(57) And they said,

"Let us call the young woman and ask אֶת her opinion."

(58) And they called Riv-kah (*Rebekah*) and said to her,

"Will you go with this man?"

And she said,

"I will go."

(59) So they sent אֵת Riv-kah (*Rebekah*) their sister וְאֶת (*and **) her nurse וְאֶת (*and **) the servant of Av-ra-ham וְאֶת (*and **) his men.

(60) And they blessed אֵת Riv-kah (*Rebekah*) and said to her,

אַתְּ (You) are our sister; may you become countless thousands; and may your seed take possession of אֵת the gate of his enemies."

(61) And Riv-kah (*Rebekah*) and her maidservants arose, and they mounted the camels and followed the man. And the servant took אֶת Riv-kah (*Rebekah*) and left.

Isaac Marries Rebekah

(62) Now Yitz-khak (*Isaac*) was coming from the direction of B'er~La-khai~Ro-i.

Level One   בְּרֵאשִׁית ~ כד

And he was living in the land of the Ne-gev.

(63) And Yitz-khak (*Isaac*) went out to meditate in the field early in the evening, and he lifted up his eyes and saw -- behold, camels were coming.

(64) And Riv-kah (*Rebekah*) lifted up אֶת her eyes and saw אֶת Yitz-khak (*Isaac*). And she fell from the camel.

(65) And she said to the servant,

> "Who is this man walking around in the field to meet us?"

And the servant said,

> "That is אֲדֹנִי (*my lord*)."

And she took her veil and covered herself.

(66) And the servant told Yitz-khak (*Isaac*) אֵת all the things that he had done.

(67) And Yitz-khak (*Isaac*) brought her to the tent of Sa-rah his mother. And he took אֶת Riv-kah (*Rebekah*), and she became his wife. And Yitz-khak (*Isaac*) loved her and was comforted after the death of his mother.

Chapter 25

Descendants Of Abraham And Keturah

(1) Now Av-ra-ham again took a wife, and her name was K'tu-rah.

(2) And she bore to him אֶת Zim-ran וְאֶת (and *) Yak-shan וְאֶת (and *) M'dan וְאֶת (and *) Mid-yan וְאֶת (and *) Yish-bak וְאֶת (and *) Shu-akh.

(3) And Yak-shan fathered אֶת Sh'va וְאֶת (and *) D'dan. And the sons of D'dan were A-shu-rim and L'tu-shim and L'um-mim.

(4) And the sons of Mid-yan were Ay-fah, Ay-fer, Kha-nokh, A-vi-dah, and El-da-ah. All of these were the children of K'tu-rah.

(5) And Av-ra-ham gave אֶת all he had to Yitz-khak (*Isaac*).

(6) But to the sons of Av-ra-ham's concubines, Av-ra-ham gave gifts. And while he was still living he sent them away eastward, away from his son Yitz-khak (*Isaac*), to the land of the east.

Death of Abraham

(7) Now these are the days of the years of the life of Av-ra-ham: a hundred and seventy-five years.

(8) And Av-ra-ham passed away and died in a טוֹבָה (*good*) old age, old and full of years. And he was gathered to his people.

(9) And Yitz-khak (*Isaac*) and Yish-ma-el his sons buried אֹתוֹ (* *him*) in the cave of Makh-pe-lah, in the field of Ef-ron, son of Zo-khar the Khit-ti (*Hittite*), that was east of Mam-re.

(10) The field that Av-ra-ham had bought מֵאֵת (*from* *) the sons of Khet, there Av-ra-ham was buried and Sa-rah his wife.

Level One   בְּרֵאשִׁית ~ כה

(11) And it happened that after the death of Av-ra-ham וַיְבָרֶךְ אֱלֹהִים (*Elohim blessed*) אֶת Yitz-khak (*Isaac*) his son, and Yitz-khak (*Isaac*) settled at B'er~La-khai~Ro-i.

Descendants Of Ishmael

(12) Now these are the generations of Yish-ma-el, the son of Av-ra-ham, that Ha-gar the Mitz-rit (*Egyptian*), the maidservant of Sa-rah, bore to Av-ra-ham.

(13-15) And these are the names of the sons of Yish-ma-el, by their names according to their family records. The firstborn of Yish-ma-el was N'va-yot, and Ke-dar, and Ad-b'el, and Miv-sam, and Mish-ma, and Du-mah, and Mas-sa, Kha-dad, and Tay-ma, Y'tur, Na-fish, and Ked-mah.

(16) These are the sons of Yish-ma-el, and these are their names by their villages and by their encampments -- twelve leaders according to their tribes.

(17) Now these are the years of the life of Yish-ma-el: a hundred and thirty-seven years. And he passed away and died, and was gathered to his people.

(18) They settled from Kha-vi-lah to Shur, which was opposite Mitz-ra-yim (*Egypt*), going toward A-shur, opposite; he settled opposite all his brothers.

Esau And Jacob Are Born

(19) Now these are the generations of Yitz-khak (*Isaac*), the son of Av-ra-ham. Av-ra-ham fathered אֶת Yitz-khak (*Isaac*),

(20) And Yitz-khak (*Isaac*) was forty years old when he took אֶת Riv-kah (*Rebekah*), the daughter of B'tu-el the A-ra-mi (*Aramean*) from Pad-dan~A-ram, the sister of La-van the A-ra-mi (*Aramean*), as his wife.

(21) And Yitz-khak (*Isaac*) prayed לַיהוה (*to YHVH*) on behalf of his wife, for

she was barren. And יהוה (*YHVH*) responded to his prayer, and Riv-kah (*Rebekah*) his wife conceived.

(22) And the children in her womb struggled against each other, and she said,

> "If it is going to be like this, why be pregnant?"

And she went to inquire of אֶת יהוה (* *YHVH*).

(23) And יהוה (*YHVH*) said to her,

> שְׁנֵי גיִים בְּבִטְנֵךְ
> וּשְׁנֵי לְאֻמִּים מִמֵּעַיִךְ יִפָּרֵדוּ
> וּלְאֹם מִלְאֹם יֶאֱמָץ
> וְרַב יַעֲבֹד צָעִיר

> Two nations are in your belly,
> and two peoples from your bowels shall be divided.
> And one people shall be stronger than the other people,
> and the much shall serve the little.

(24) And when her days to give birth were completed then behold, twins were in her womb.

(25) And the first came out red, all his body was like a coat of שֵׂעָר (*hair*), so they called his name עֵשָׂו (*Esau*).

(26) And afterward his brother came out, and his hand grasped בַּעֲקֵב (*on the heel*) of E-sav, so his name was called יַעֲקֹב (*Jacob*). And Yitz-khak (*Isaac*) was sixty years old when she bore אֹתָם (* *them*).

(27) And the boys grew up. And E-sav was a skilled hunter, a man of the field, but Ya-a-kov (*Jacob*) was a peaceful man, living in tents.

Level One

בְּרֵאשִׁית ~ כה

(28) And Yitz-khak (*Isaac*) loved אֶת E-sav because he could eat of his game, but Riv-kah (*Rebekah*) loved אֶת Ya-a-kov (*Jacob*).

Esau Sales His Birthright

(29) Once Ya-a-kov (*Jacob*) cooked a thick stew, and E-sav came in from the field, and he was exhausted.

(30) And E-sav said to Ya-a-kov (*Jacob*),

> *"Please, give me some of that red stuff to gulp down, for I am exhausted!"*

Therefore, his name was called E-dom.

(31) Then Ya-a-kov (*Jacob*) said,

> *"Sell as of today your* אֶת *birthright to me."*

(32) And E-sav said,

> *"Look, I am going to die; now what is this birthright to me?"*

(33) Then Ya-a-kov (*Jacob*) said,

> *"Swear to me as of today."*

And he swore to him, and sold אֶת his birthright to Ya-a-kov (*Jacob*).

(34) And Ya-a-kov (*Jacob*) gave E-sav bread and lentil stew, and he ate and drank. Then he got up and went away. And E-sav despised אֶת his birthright.

Chapter 26

Isaac Goes To Gerar

(1) And there was a famine in the land, besides the former famine which was in the days of Av-ra-ham. And Yitz-khak (*Isaac*) went to A-vi-me-lech, king of the P'lish-tim (*Philistines*), to G'rar.

(2) וַיֵּרָא אֵלָיו יהוה (*And YHVH appeared*) to him וַיֹּאמֶר (*and He said*)

אַל־תֵּרֵד מִצְרָיְמָה

שְׁכֹן בָּאָרֶץ

אֲשֶׁר אֹמַר אֵלֶיךָ

Do not go down toward Egypt;
tabernacle in the land
which I am saying to you.

(3)

גּוּר בָּאָרֶץ הַזֹּאת

וְאֶהְיֶה עִמְּךָ וַאֲבָרְכֶךָ

כִּכִּי־לְךָ וּלְזַרְעֲךָ

אֶתֵּן אֶת־כָּל־הָאֲרָצֹת הָאֵל

Sojourn in this land,
and I will be with you, and will bless you,
for to you and to your seed
I will give * all these lands,

Level One בְּרֵאשִׁית ~ כו

וַהֲקִמֹתִי אֶת-הַשְּׁבֻעָה
אֲשֶׁר נִשְׁבַּעְתִּי לְאַבְרָהָם אָבִיךָ

and I will carry out * the oath
that I swore to Abraham your father.

(4)

וְהִרְבֵּיתִי אֶת-זַרְעֲךָ
כְּכוֹכְבֵי הַשָּׁמַיִם
וְנָתַתִּי לְזַרְעֲךָ
אֵת כָּל-הָאֲרָצֹת הָאֵל
וְהִתְבָּרְכוּ בְזַרְעֲךָ
כֹּל גּוֹיֵי הָאָרֶץ

And I will increase * your seed
like the stars of the sky,
and I will give to your seed
* all these lands.
And they will be blessed in your seed --
all the nations of the land"

(5)

עֵקֶב אֲשֶׁר-שָׁמַע אַבְרָהָם בְּקֹלִי
וַיִּשְׁמֹר מִשְׁמַרְתִּי מִצְוֹתַי

Inasmuch that Abraham heard in My voice
and kept My charge, My commandments,

Genesis ~ 26

חֻקּוֹתַי וְתוֹרֹתָי

My statutes, and My instructions.

(6) So Yitz-khak (*Isaac*) settled in G'rar.

(7) When the men of the place asked concerning his wife, he said,

"She is my sister,"

for he was afraid to say,

"She is my wife,"

lest

"the men of the place will kill me on account of Riv-kah (*Rebekah*),"

for she was טוֹבַת (*good of*) appearance.

(8) And it happened that, when he had been there a long time, A-vi-me-lech the king of the P'lish-tim (*Philistines*) looked through the window, and saw behold, Yitz-khak (*Isaac*) was jesting with אֶת Riv-kah (*Rebekah*) his wife.

(9) And A-vi-me-lech called Yitz-khak (*Isaac*) and said,

"Surely she is your wife. Now why did you say

'She is my sister,'?"

And Yitz-khak (*Isaac*) said to him,

"Because I thought I would die on account of her."

(10) And A-vi-me-lech said,

"What is this you have done to us? One of the people might easily

Level One

בְּרֵאשִׁית ~ כו

have slept with אֵת *your wife! Then you would have brought guilt upon us!"*

(11) Then A-vi-me-lech instructed אֵת all the people, saying,

"The one who touches this man or his wife shall certainly die."

Isaac Prospers

(12) And Yitz-khak (*Isaac*) sowed in that land and reaped in that same year a hundredfold וַיְבָרְכֵהוּ יהוה (*and YHVH blessed him*) .

(13) And the man became wealthier and wealthier until he was exceedingly wealthy.

(14) And he possessed sheep and cattle and many servants, and the P'lish-tim (*Philistines*) envied אֹתוֹ (* *him*).

(15) And the P'lish-tim (*Philistines*) stopped up all the wells that the servants of his father had dug in the days of Av-ra-ham his father. They filled them with soil.

(16) And A-vi-me-lech said to Yitz-khak (*Isaac*),

"Go away from us, for you have become much too powerful for us."

(17) So Yitz-khak (*Isaac*) departed from there and camped in the valley of G'rar, and settled there.

Quarreling Over The Wells

(18) And Yitz-khak (*Isaac*) dug again אֵת the wells of water which they had dug in the days of his father Av-ra-ham, which the P'lish-tim (*Philistines*) had stopped up after the death of Av-ra-ham. And he gave to them the same names which his father had given them.

(19) And when the servants of Yitz-khak (*Isaac*) dug in the valley, they found a well of fresh water there.

(20) Then רֹעֵי גְרָר (*the shepherds of Gerar*) quarreled with רֹעֵי יִצְחָק (*the shepherds of Isaac*), saying,

"*The water is ours.*"

And he called the name of the well E-sek, because they contended with him.

(21) And they dug another well, and they quarreled over it also. And he called its name Sit-nah.

(22) Then he moved from there and dug another well, and they did not quarrel over it. And he called its name R'kho-vot, and said,

"*Now* יהוה *(YHVH) has made room for us, and we shall be fruitful in the land.*"

(23) And from there he went up to Ber~Sha-va.

(24) וַיֵּרָא יהוה (*And YHVH appeared*) to him that night וַיֹּאמֶר (*and He said*)

אָנֹכִי אֱלֹהֵי אַבְרָהָם אָבִיךָ

אַל־תִּירָא

כִּי־אִתְּךָ אָנֹכִי

I am the Elohim of Abraham your father.
You must not fear,
*because I am with * you,*

וּבֵרַכְתִּיךָ וְהִרְבֵּיתִי אֶת־זַרְעֲךָ

בַּעֲבוּר אַבְרָהָם עַבְדִּי

150

Level One

בְּרֵאשִׁית ~ כו

and I will bless you and will increase * your seed

on account of Abraham My servant.

(25) And he built an altar there and called on the name of יהוה (*YHVH*). And he pitched his tent there, and the servants of Yitz-khak (*Isaac*) dug a well there.

Isaac Covenants With Abimelech

(26) Then A-vi-me-lech went to him from G'rar, and A-khuz-zat his friend and Fi-khol, commander of his army.

(27) And Yitz-khak (*Isaac*) said to them,

> "Why have you come to me? You hate אֹתִי (** me*) and sent me away מֵאִתְּכֶם (*from * you*)."

(28) And they said,

> "We see clearly that יהוה (*YHVH*) has been with you. And we say,
>
> > 'Please, let there be an oath between us -- between us and you -- and let us make a covenant with you.'"

(29)

> "You should not do us רָעָה (*evil*) just as we have not touched you, but have only done טוֹב (*good*) to you and sent you away בְּשָׁלוֹם (*in peace*). אַתָּה (*You*) are now being blessed of יהוה (*YHVH*)."

(30) So he made a meal for them, and they ate and drank.

(31) And they arose early in the morning and each one swore to the other, and Yitz-khak (*Isaac*) sent them away. And they left מֵאִתּוֹ (*from * him*) בְּשָׁלוֹם (*in peace*).

Genesis ~ 26

(32) And it happened that on that same day the servants of Yitz-khak (*Isaac*) came and told him about the well that they had dug. And they said,

"*We have found water!*"

(33) And he called אֹתָה (** it*) Shiv-a. Therefore, the name of the city is Ber~She-va unto this day.

Esau Marries

(34) And when E-sav was forty years old he took as wife אֶת Y'hu-dit, daughter of B'e-ri the Khit-ti (*Hittite*) וְאֶת (*and **) Bas-mat, daughter of Ay-lon the Khit-ti (*Hittite*).

(35) And they became bitterness of רוּחַ (*spirit*) for Yitz-khak (*Isaac*) and Riv-kah (*Rebekah*).

Chapter 27

Jacob Steals The Blessing

(1) And it happened that when Yitz-khak (*Isaac*) was old and his eyesight was weak, he called אֶת E-sav his older son and said to him,

> "*My son.*"

And he said to him,

> "*Here I am.*"

(2) And he said,

> "*Look, I am old; I do not know the day of my death.*"

(3)

> "*And now, take your weapons, your quiver and your bow, and go out to the field and hunt food for me.*"

(4)

> "*And make for me tasty food like I love, and bring it to me. And I will eat it so that I can bless you before I die.*"

(5) Now Riv-kah (*Rebekah*) was listening as Yitz-khak (*Isaac*) spoke to E-sav his son, and when E-sav went to the field to hunt wild game to bring back,

(6) Riv-kah (*Rebekah*) said to Ya-a-kov (*Jacob*) her son,

> "*Look, I heard* אֶת *your father speaking to E-sav your brother saying,*

(7)
> 'Bring wild game to me and prepare tasty food so I can eat it and bless you before יהוה (YHVH) before my death.' "

(8)
> "And now, my son, listen to my voice, to what I instruct אֹתָךְ (* you)."

(9)
> "Go to the flock and take two טֹבִים (good) young goats from it for me, and I will prepare אֹתָם (* them) tasty for your father, just as he loves."

(10)
> "And you bring it to your father and he will eat it in order that he may bless you before his death."

(11) Then Ya-a-kov (Jacob) said to his mother,

> "Behold, E-sav my brother is a hairy man, and I am a smooth man."

(12)
> "Perhaps my father will feel me and I will be in his eyes as a mocker, and I bring on me a curse and not a blessing."

(13) Then his mother said to him,

> "Your curse be upon me, my son, only listen to my voice -- go and get them for me."

(14) So he went and took them, and brought them to his mother, and his mother prepared tasty food as his father liked.

(15) Then Riv-kah (*Rebekah*) took אֵת garments of her older son E-sav -- the

Level One   בְּרֵאשִׁית ~ כז

coveted ones that were with אִתָּהּ (* her) in the house, and she put them on אֶת Ya-a-kov (Jacob) her younger son.

(16) וְאֵת (and *) the skins of the young goats she put over his hands and over the smooth part of his neck.

(17) And she put אֶת the tasty food וְאֶת (and *) the bread that she had made into the hand of Ya-a-kov (Jacob), her son.

(18) And he went to his father and said,

> "My father."

And he said,

> "Here I am. Who are אַתָּה (you), my son?"

(19) And Ya-a-kov (Jacob) said to his father,

> "I am E-sav, your firstborn. I have done as you told me. Please get up, sit up and eat from my wild game in order that you may bless me."

(20) Then Yitz-khak (Isaac) said to his son,

> "How did you find it so quickly, my son?"

And he said,

> "Because יהוה אֱלֹהֶיךָ (YHVH, your Elohim) caused me to find it."

(21) Then Yitz-khak (Isaac) said to Ya-a-kov (Jacob),

> "Please, come near and let me feel you, my son. Are you really my son E-sav or not?"

Genesis ~ 27

(22) And Ya-a-kov (*Jacob*) drew near to Yitz-khak (*Isaac*) his father. And he felt him and said,

> "The voice is the voice of Ya-a-kov (*Jacob*), but the hands are the hands of E-sav."

(23) And he did not recognize him because his hands were hairy like the hands of E-sav his brother. And he blessed him.

(24) And he said,

> "Are אַתָּה (*you*) really my son E-sav?"

And he said,

> "I am."

(25) Then he said,

> "Bring it near to me that I may eat from the game of my son, so that I may bless you."

And he brought it to him, and he ate. And he brought wine him, and he drank.

(26) Then his father Yitz-khak (*Isaac*) said to him,

> "Come near and kiss me, my son."

(27) And he drew near and kissed him. And he smelled אֶת the smell of his garments, and he blessed him and said,

> "Look, the smell of my son is like the smell of a field that בֵּרְכוֹ יהוה (*YHVH has blessed*)."

(28)

> וְיִתֶּן הָאֱלֹהִים (*the Elohim give*) you of the dew of the sky and of the

Level One
בְּרֵאשִׁית ~ כז

> fatness of the land, and abundance of grain and new wine."

(29)
> "Let peoples serve you, and nations bow down to you; Be a ruler to your brothers, and may the sons of your mother bow down to you. Cursed be those cursing you, and blessed be those blessing you."

Esau Returns

(30) And as soon as Yitz-khak (*Isaac*) had finished blessing אֶת Ya-a-kov (*Jacob*), immediately after Ya-a-kov (*Jacob*) had gone out מֵאֵת (*from **) the presence of Yitz-khak (*Isaac*) his father, E-sav his brother came back from his hunting.

(31) He too prepared tasty food and brought it to his father. And he said to his father,

> "Let my father arise and eat from the wild game of his son, that you may bless me."

(32) And Yitz-khak (*Isaac*) his father said to him,

> "Who are אַתָּה (*you*)?"

And he said,

> "I am your son, your firstborn, E-sav."

(33) Then Yitz-khak (*Isaac*) trembled violently. Then he said,

> "Who then was he that hunted wild game and brought it to me, and I ate it all before you came, and I blessed him? Moreover, he will be blessed!"

(34) When E-sav heard אֶת the words of his father he cried out with a great and exceedingly bitter cry of distress. And he said to his father,

> "Bless me as well, my father!"

(35) And he said,

> "Your brother came in deceit and took your blessing."

(36) Then he said,

> "Isn't that why he is named Ya-a-kov (Jacob)? He has deceived me these two times. He took אֶת my birthright and look, now he has taken my blessing!"

Then he said,
> "Have you not reserved a blessing for me?"

(37) Then Yitz-khak (Isaac) answered and said to E-sav,

> "Behold, I have made him ruler over you וְאֶת (and *) all his brothers I have given him as servants, and with grain and wine I have sustained him. And what can I do for you, my son?"

(38) And E-sav said to his father,

> "Have you only one blessing, my father? Bless me also, my father!"

And E-sav lifted up his voice and wept.

(39) Then Yitz-khak (Isaac) his father answered and said to him,

> "Your home shall be from the fatness of the land, and from the dew

Level One   בְּרֵאשִׁית ~ כז

of the sky above."

(40)

"And on your sword you shall live וְאֶת *(and *) your brother you shall serve. And it shall be that when you become restless then you will break off his yoke from your neck."*

Esau Threatens to Kill Jacob

(41) Then E-sav held a grudge against אֶת Ya-a-kov (*Jacob*) on account of the blessing with which his father had blessed him. And E-sav said in his heart,

"The days of mourning for my father are coming, then I will kill אֶת *Ya-a-kov (Jacob) my brother."*

(42) And אֶת the words of E-sav her older son were told to Riv-kah (*Rebekah*). And she sent and called for her younger son Ya-a-kov (*Jacob*). And she said to him,

"Look, E-sav your brother is consoling himself concerning you, intending to kill you."

(43)

"Now then, my son, listen to my voice; arise and flee to Ha-ran to La-van my brother."

(44)

"Stay with him a few days until the wrath of your brother has turned."

(45)

"Until the anger of your brother turns from you and he אֶת *forgets what you have done to him. Then I will send and bring you from*

there. Why should I lose the two of you in one day?"

(46) Then Riv-kah (Rebekah) said to Yitz-khak (Isaac),

"I am irritated in my life because of the daughters of Khet. If Ya-a-kov (Jacob) takes a wife from the daughters of Khet like these from the daughters of the land, what am I living for?"

Chapter 28

Jacob Leaves Home

(1) Then Yitz-khak (*Isaac*) called Ya-a-kov (*Jacob*) and blessed אֹתוֹ (* him). And he instructed him and said to him,

> "You must not take a wife from the daughters of K'na-an."

(2)

> "Arise, go to Pad-de-nah~A-ram, to the house of B'tu-el, your mother's father, and take for yourself a wife from there, from the daughters of La-van your mother's brother."

(3)

> וְאֵל שַׁדַּי יְבָרֵךְ (And El Almighty bless) אֹתְךָ (* you), and make you fruitful, and multiply you, so that you become an assembly of peoples."

(4)

> וְיִתֶּן (And may He give) to you אֶת-בִּרְכַּת אַבְרָהָם (* the blessing of Av-ra-ham), to you and to your seed with אִתָּךְ (* you), that you may take possession of אֵת the land of your sojourning, which נָתַן אֱלֹהִים (Elohim gave) to Av-ra-ham."

(5) Then Yitz-khak (*Isaac*) sent אֶת Ya-a-kov (*Jacob*) away, and he went to Pad-de-nah~A-ram, to La-van the son of the A-ra-mi (*Aramean*), the brother of Riv-kah (*Rebekah*), the mother of Ya-a-kov (*Jacob*) and E-sav.

(6) Now E-sav saw that Yitz-khak (*Isaac*) had blessed אֶת Ya-a-kov (*Jacob*) and sent אֹתוֹ (* him) away to Pad-de-nah~A-ram, to take for himself a wife from there, and he blessed אֹתוֹ (* him) and instructed him, saying,

"You must not take a wife from the daughters of K'na-an,"

(7) and that Ya-a-kov (*Jacob*) listened to his father and to his mother and went to Pad-de-nah~A-ram.

Esau Marries Ishmael's Daughter

(8) And E-sav saw that the daughters of K'na-an were רָעוֹת (*evil ones*) in the eyes of Yitz-khak (*Isaac*) his father.

(9) And E-sav went to Yish-ma-el and took אֶת Ma-kha-lat, the daughter of Yish-ma-el, son of Av-ra-ham, sister of N'va-yot, as a wife, in addition to the wives he had.

The Ladder

(10) Then Ya-a-kov (*Jacob*) went out from Ber~Sha-va and went to Ha-ran.

(11) And he arrived at a certain place and spent the night there, because the sun had set. And he took one of the stones of the place and put it under his head and slept at that place.

(12) And he dreamed, and behold, a stairway was set on the land, and its top touched the sky. And behold מַלְאֲכֵי אֱלֹהִים (*messengers of Elohim*) עֹלִים וְיֹרְדִים (*ascending ones and descending ones*) on it.

(13) And behold יהוה נִצָּב (*YHVH was stationed*) beside him וַיֹּאמַר (*and He said*)

אֲנִי יהוה

אֱלֹהֵי אַבְרָהָם אָבִיךָ

וֵאלֹהֵי יִצְחָק

Level One

בְּרֵאשִׁית ~ כח

I am YHVH
the Elohim of Abraham your father,
and the Elohim of Isaac.

הָאָרֶץ אֲשֶׁר אַתָּה שֹׁכֵב עָלֶיהָ
לְךָ אֶתְּנֶנָּה וּלְזַרְעֶךָ

The land on which you lie down
I will give to you and to your seed.

(14)

וְהָיָה זַרְעֲךָ כַּעֲפַר הָאָרֶץ
וּפָרַצְתָּ יָמָּה וָקֵדְמָה
וְצָפֹנָה וָנֶגְבָּה
וְנִבְרְכוּ בְךָ
כָּל־מִשְׁפְּחֹת הָאֲדָמָה
וּבְזַרְעֶךָ

Your seed shall be like the soil of the land,
and you will spread out seaward, and eastward,
and northward and southward.
And they are blessed in you –
all the families of the ground --
and in your seed.

(15)

וְהִנֵּה אָנֹכִי עִמָּךְ

And behold, I am with you,

Genesis ~ 28

וּשְׁמַרְתִּ֙יךָ֙ בְּכֹ֣ל

אֲשֶׁר־תֵּלֵ֔ךְ

וַהֲשִׁבֹתִ֖יךָ אֶל־הָאֲדָמָ֣ה הַזֹּ֑את

כִּ֚י לֹ֣א אֶֽעֱזָבְךָ֔

עַ֚ד אֲשֶׁ֣ר אִם־עָשִׂ֔יתִי

אֵ֥ת אֲשֶׁר־דִּבַּ֖רְתִּי לָֽךְ

and I will keep you in all
which you go.
And I will bring you to this ground,
because I will not depart from you
until I have done
* what I spoke to you.

Jacob Vows To Elohim

(16) Then Ya-a-kov (*Jacob*) awoke from his sleep and said,

"Surely יהוה (*YHVH*) is indeed in this place and I did not know!"

(17) And he was afraid and said,

"How awesome is this place! This is nothing else than the House of אֱלֹהִים (*Elohim*), and this is the gate of the sky!"

(18) And Ya-a-kov (*Jacob*) rose early in the morning, and he took אֶת the stone that he had put under his head and set אֹתָהּ (* *it*) up as a stone pillar, and poured oil on top of it.

Level One   בְּרֵאשִׁית ~ כח

(19) And he called אֵת the name of that place בֵּית-אֵל (*Bet-El / the house of El*); however, the name of the city was formerly Luz.

(20) And Ya-a-kov (*Jacob*) made a vow saying,

    "If יִהְיֶה אֱלֹהִים (*Elohim will be*) with me and protect me on this way that I am going, and gives me food to eat and clothing to wear,

(21)

    "and I return בְשָׁלוֹם (*in peace*) to the house of my father, then וְהָיָה יהוה (*YHVH will be*) לֵאלֹהִים (*for Elohim*) to me."

(22)

    "And this stone that I have set up as a pillar shall be the House of אֱלֹהִים (*Elohim*) and of all that You give to me I will certainly give a tenth to You."

Chapter 29

Jacob Meets Rachel

(1) And Ya-a-kov (*Jacob*) continued his journey and went toward the land of the sons of the east.

(2) And he looked, and behold, there was a well in the field, and behold, there were three flocks of sheep lying beside it, for out of that well the flocks were watered. And the stone on the mouth of the well was large.

(3) And when all the flocks were gathered there, they rolled אֶת the stone from the mouth of the well. And they watered אֶת the sheep and returned אֶת the stone upon the mouth of the well to its place.

(4) And Ya-a-kov (Jacob) said to them,

"My brothers, where are אַתֶּם *(you) from?*"

And they said,

"*We are from Ha-ran.*"

(5) And he said to them,

"*Do you know* אֶת *La-van, son of Na-khor?*"

And they said,

"*We know him.*"

(6) And he said to them,

הֲשָׁלוֹם *(The peace) for him?*"

And they said,

שָׁלוֹם (Shalom). Now look, Ra-khel his daughter is coming with the sheep."

(7) And he said,

"Look, it is still broad daylight; it is not the time for the livestock to be gathered. Give water to the sheep and go, pasture them."

(8) And they said,

"We are not able until all the flocks are gathered and they roll אֶת the stone from the mouth of the well, and we water the sheep."

(9) While he was speaking with them, Ra-khel came with the sheep which belonged to her father, for she was רֹעָה (a shepherdess).

(10) And it happened that, when Ya-a-kov (Jacob) saw אֶת Ra-khel, the daughter of La-van, his mother's brother וְאֶת (and *) the flock of La-van, his mother's brother, Ya-a-kov (Jacob) drew near and rolled אֶת the stone from the mouth of the well and watered אֶת the flock of La-van, his mother's brother.

(11) And Ya-a-kov (*Jacob*) kissed Ra-khel, and lifted up אֶת his voice and wept.

(12) And Ya-a-kov (*Jacob*) told Ra-khel that he was the relative of her father, and that he was the son of Riv-kah (*Rebekah*). And she ran and told her father.

Jacob Meets Laban

(13) And it happened that when La-van heard אֶת the report about Ya-a-kov (Jacob), the son of his sister, he ran to meet him. And he embraced him and kissed him, and brought him to his house. And he told La-van אֶת all these things.

(14) And La-van said to him,

> "Surely אַתָּה (you) are my flesh and my bone!"

And he stayed with him a month of days.

(15) Then La-van said to Ya-a-kov (Jacob),

> "Just because אַתָּה (you) are my brother should you work for me for nothing? Tell me what your wage should be."

(16) Now La-van had two daughters. The name of the older was Le-ah, and the name of the younger was Ra-khel.

(17) Now the eyes of Le-ah were tender, and Ra-khel was beautiful in shape and appearance.

(18) And Ya-a-kov (*Jacob*) loved אֶת Ra-khel and said,

> "I will serve you seven years for Ra-khel your younger daughter."

(19) Then La-van said,

> טוֹב (Good) that I give אֹתָהּ (* her) to you than I give אֹתָהּ (* her) to another man. Dwell with me."

(20) And Ya-a-kov (*Jacob*) worked for Ra-khel seven years, but they were as a few days in his eyes because of his love of אֹתָהּ (* her).

Laban Tricks Jacob

(21) And Ya-a-kov (Jacob) said to La-van,

> "Give me אֶת my wife, that I may go in to her, for my time is completed."

Level One

בְּרֵאשִׁית ~ כט

(22) So La-van gathered אֵת all the men of the place and prepared a feast.

(23) And it happened that in the evening he took אֵת Le-ah his daughter and brought אֹתָהּ (* her) to him, and he went in to her.

(24) And La-van gave אֵת Zil-pah his female servant to her, to Le-ah his daughter, as a female servant.

(25) And it happened that in the morning, behold, it was Le-ah! And he said to La-van,

> "What is this you have done to me? Did I not serve with you for Ra-khel? Now why did you deceive me?"

(26) Then La-van said,

> "It is not the custom in our country to give the younger before the firstborn."

(27)

> "Complete the week of this one, then I will also give you אֵת the other, on the condition that you will work for me another seven years."

(28) And Ya-a-kov (*Jacob*) did so. So he completed the week of this one, then he gave אֵת Ra-khel his daughter to him as a wife.

(29) And La-van gave אֵת Bil-hah his female servant to Ra-khel his daughter as a female servant.

(30) And he also went in to Ra-khel, and he also loved אֵת Ra-khel more than Le-ah. And he served with him yet another seven years.

Sons Of Leah

(31) וַיַּרְא יהוה (And YHVH saw) that Le-ah was hated וַיִּפְתַּח (and He opened) אֶת her womb, but Ra-khel was barren.

(32) Then Le-ah conceived and gave birth to a son, and she called his name רְאוּבֵן (Reuben), for she said,

> "Because רָאָה יהוה (YHVH saw) my misery, that I am unloved. Now my husband will love me."

(33) And she conceived again and gave birth to a son. And she said,

> "It is because שָׁמַע יהוה (YHVH heard) that I am hated וַיִּתֶּן (and He gave) me אֶת this one also."

And she called his name שִׁמְעוֹן (Simeon).

(34) And she conceived again and gave birth to a son. And she said,

> "Now this time my husband יִלָּוֶה (he will be obligated) to me, because I have borne for him three sons."

Therefore, he called his name לֵוִי (Levi.)

(35) And she conceived again and gave birthed a son. And she said,

> "This time אוֹדֶה (I will praise) אֶת יהוה (* YHVH)."

Therefore, she called his name יְהוּדָה (Judah). And she ceased bearing children.

Chapter 30

Sons Of Bilhah

(1) When Ra-khel saw that she could not bear children to Ya-a-kov (*Jacob*), Ra-khel envied her sister. And she said to Ya-a-kov (*Jacob*),

> "Give me children if not, I will die!"

(2) And Ya-a-kov (*Jacob*) became angry with Ra-khel. And he said,

> "Am I in the place of אֱלֹהִים (*Elohim*) Who has withheld from you the fruit of the womb?"

(3) Then she said,

> "Here is my maidservant Bil-hah; go in to her that she may bear children as my surrogate. Then I will even have children by her."

(4) Then she gave him אֵת Bil-hah, her female servant, for a wife, and Ya-a-kov (*Jacob*) went in to her

(5) And Bil-hah conceived and gave birth to a son for Ya-a-kov (*Jacob*).

(6) Then Ra-khel said,

> דָּנַנִּי אֱלֹהִים (*Elohim has adjudicated me*), and also שָׁמַע (*He heard*) my voice וַיִּתֶּן (*and he gave*) me a son."

Therefore, she called his name דָּן (*Dan*).

(7) And Bil-hah, Ra-khel's servant, conceived again and bore a second son to Ya-a-kov (*Jacob*).

Genesis ~ 30

(8) And Ra-khel said,

> With נַפְתּוּלֵי אֱלֹהִים (wrestlings of Elohim) נִפְתַּלְתִּי (I have wrestled) with my sister and also I prevailed."

And she called his name נַפְתָּלִי (Naphtali).

Sons Of Zilpah

(9) When Le-ah saw that she had ceased bearing children, she took אֶת Zil-pah her female servant and gave אֹתָהּ (* her) to Ya-a-kov (Jacob) for a wife.

(10) And Zil-pah, the female slave of Le-ah, bore a son to Ya-a-kov (Jacob).

(11) Then Le-ah said,

> בָּא גָד (A troop comes)!"

And she called אֶת his name גָּד (Gad).

(12) And Zil-pah, Le-ah's female servant, bore a second son to Ya-a-kov (Jacob).

(13) Then Le-ah said,

> בְּאָשְׁרִי (I am in happiness) For women אִשְּׁרוּנִי (have called me happy)."

So she called אֶת his name אָשֵׁר (Asher).

More Sons Of Leah

(14) And in the days of the wheat harvest, R'u-ven went and found mandrakes in the field and he brought אֹתָם (* them) to Le-ah his mother. And Ra-khel said to Le-ah,

Level One   בְּרֵאשִׁית ~ ל

> "Please give me some of your son's mandrakes."

(15) And she said to her,

> "Is your taking אֶת my husband such a small thing that you will also take אֶת the mandrakes of my son?"

And Ra-khel said,

> "Then he may sleep with you tonight in exchange for your son's mandrakes."

(16) When Ya-a-kov (*Jacob*) came in from the field in the evening, Le-ah went out to meet him. And she said,

> "Come in to me, for I have hired you with my son's mandrakes."

And he slept with her that night.

(17) וַיִּשְׁמַע אֱלֹהִים (*And Elohim listened*) to Le-ah and she conceived and gave birth to a fifth son for Ya-a-kov (*Jacob*).

(18) Then Le-ah said,

> נָתַן אֱלֹהִים (*Elohim gave*) me שְׂכָרִי (*my wage*) since I gave my servant girl to my husband."

And she called his name יִשָּׂשכָר (*Issachar*).

(19) And Le-ah conceived again and gave birth to a sixth son for Ya-a-kov (*Jacob*).

(20) And Le-ah said,

> זְבָדַנִי אֱלֹהִים (*Elohim endowed*) אֹתִי (* *me*) with a טוֹב (*good*) dowry. This time my husband יִזְבְּלֵנִי (*he will prefer me*), because I

Genesis ~ 30

bore him six sons."

And she called אֶת his name (Zebulun).

(21) And afterward she gave birth to a daughter. And she called אֶת her name Di-nah.

The Birth Of Joseph

(22) וַיִּשְׁמַע אֱלֹהִים וַיִּזְכֹּר אֱלֹהִים (And Elohim remembered) אֶת Ra-khel (and Elohim listened) to her וַיִּפְתַּח (and He opened) אֶת her womb.

(23) And she conceived and gave birth to a son. And she said,

אָסַף אֱלֹהִים (Elohim has taken away) אֶת my disgrace."

(24) And she called אֶת his name Yo-sef, saying,

יֹסֵף יהוה (YHVH has added) to me another son."

Jacob Wants To Leave Laban

(25) And it happened that as soon as Ra-khel had given birthed אֶת Yo-sef, Ya-a-kov (*Jacob*) said to La-van,

> "Send me away that I may go to my place and my land."

(26)

> "Give me אֶת my wives וְאֶת (and *) my children for which I have served אֹתְךָ (* you), and let me go. For אַתָּה (you) yourself know אֶת my service that I have rendered to you."

Level One   בְּרֵאשִׁית ~ ל

(27) But La-van said to him,

> "Please, if I have found favor in your eyes, I have seen the signs that וַיְבָרְכֵנִי יהוה (YHVH has blessed me) because of you."

(28) And he said,

> "Name your wage to me and I will give it."

(29) Then he said to him,

> אַתָּה (You) yourself know אֵת that I have served you וְאֵת (and *) that your livestock have been with אִתִּי (* me)."

(30)

> "For you had little before me, and it has increased abundantly. And וַיְבָרֶךְ יהוה (YHVH has blessed) אֹתְךָ (* you) wherever I turned. When shall I provide also for my own family?"

(31) And he said,

> "What shall I give you?"

And Ya-a-kov (Jacob) said,

> "Do not give me anything. If you will do this thing for me, I will again feed your flocks and keep them."

(32)

> "Let me pass through all your flocks today, removing all the speckled and spotted sheep from them, along with every dark-colored sheep among the sheep, and the spotted and speckled among the goats. That shall be my wages."

Genesis ~ 30

(33)

"And my righteousness will answer for me later when you come concerning my wages before you. Every one that is not speckled or spotted among the goats, or dark-colored among the sheep shall be stolen if it is with אִתִּי (* me)."

(34) Then La-van said,

"Look! Very well. It shall be according to your word."

(35) And in that day, he removed the אֶת bucks, streaked and spotted ones וְאֵת (*and **) all the she-goats, speckled and spotted ones, all that had white on it, and every dark-colored ram, and put them in the charge of his sons.

(36) And he put a journey of three days between him and Ya-a-kov (*Jacob*), and Ya-a-kov (*Jacob*) רֹעֶה (*shepherded*) La-van's אֶת flock.

Streaked, Speckled and Spotted

(37) Then Ya-a-kov (*Jacob*) took fresh branches of poplar, almond, and plane trees and peeled white strips on them, exposing the white which was on the branches.

(38) And he put אֶת the branches that he had peeled in front of the flocks, in the troughs and in the water containers. And they were in heat when they came to drink.

(39) And the flocks mated by the branches, so the flocks bore streaked, speckled, and spotted.

(40) And Ya-a-kov (*Jacob*) separated the lambs and turned the faces of the flocks toward the streaked and all the dark-colored in La-van's flocks. And he put

בְּרֵאשִׁית ~ ל

Level One

his own herds apart, and did not put them with the flocks of La-van.

(41) And whenever any of the stronger of the flocks were in heat, Ya-a-kov (Jacob) put אֶת the branches in full view of the flock in the troughs that they might mate in the branches.

(42) But with the more feeble of the flock he would not put them there. So the feebler were La-van's and the stronger were Ya-a-kov's (Jacob).

(43) And the man became exceedingly rich and had large flocks, female servants, male servants, camels, and donkeys.

Chapter 31

YHVH Tells Jacob To Return

(1) Now he heard אֵת the words of the sons of La-van, saying,

> "Ya-a-kov (*Jacob*) has taken אֵת all that our father has, and from that which was our father's he has gained אֵת all this wealth."

(2) Then Ya-a-kov (*Jacob*) saw אֵת the face of La-van and, behold, it was not like it had been in the past.

(3) וַיֹּאמֶר יהוה (*And YHVH said*) to Ya-a-kov (*Jacob*),

> שׁוּב אֶל־אֶרֶץ אֲבוֹתֶיךָ
> וּלְמוֹלַדְתֶּךָ
> וְאֶהְיֶה עִמָּךְ
>
> *Return to the land of your fathers*
> *and to your kindred,*
> *and I will be with you.*

(4) So Ya-a-kov (*Jacob*) sent and called Ra-khel and Le-ah to the field, to his flocks,

(5) and he said to them,

> "Look, I see אֵת the face of your father, that it is not like it has been toward me in the past וֵאלֹהֵי אָבִי הָיָה (*and the Elohim of my father is*) *with me.*"

Level One   בְּרֵאשִׁית ~ לֹא

(6)

"And you yourselves know that I have served אֶת your father with all my strength."

(7)

"And your father has cheated me and changed אֶת my wages ten times וְלֹא-נְתָנוֹ אֱלֹהִים (and Elohim has not allowed him) to harm me."

(8)

"If thus he said,

'Speckled shall be your wage,'

"Then all the flock bore speckled. And if he said,

'Streaked shall be your wage,'

"Then all the flock bore streaked."

(9)

וַיַּצֵּל אֱלֹהִים (And Elohim has taken away) אֶת the livestock of your father וַיִּתֶּן (and He has given them) to me."

(10)

"And it happened that at the time of the mating of the flock I lifted up my eyes and saw in a dream, and behold, the rams mounting the flock were streaked, speckled, and dappled."

(11)

וַיֹּאמֶר מַלְאַךְ הָאֱלֹהִים (And the messenger of the Elohim said) to me in the dream,

Jacob ~ יַעֲקֹב

Genesis ~ 31

"And I said,

'Here I am.' "

(12) וַיֹּאמֶר (And He said)

שָׂא-נָא עֵינֶיךָ וּרְאֵה
כָּל-הָעַתֻּדִים
הָעֹלִים עַל-הַצֹּאן
עֲקֻדִּים נְקֻדִּים וּבְרֻדִּים
כִּי רָאִיתִי אֵת כָּל
אֲשֶׁר לָבָן עֹשֶׂה לָּךְ

Please lift up your eyes and see --
all the rams,
the ones going up on the flock,
striped ones, speckled ones, and dappled ones,
because I have seen * all
that Lavan is doing to you.

(13)

אָנֹכִי הָאֵל בֵּית-אֵל
אֲשֶׁר מָשַׁחְתָּ שָּׁם מַצֵּבָה
אֲשֶׁר נָדַרְתָּ לִּי שָׁם נֶדֶר

I am the El of Bet-El / the house of El
where you anointed there a monument,
where you vowed to Me there a vow.

Level One

בְּרֵאשִׁית ~ לֹא

עַתָּה קוּם צֵא
מִן-הָאָרֶץ הַזֹּאת
וְשׁוּב אֶל-אֶרֶץ מוֹלַדְתֶּךָ

Now get up, go out
from this land
and return to the land of your kindred

(14) Then Ra-khel and Le-ah answered and said to him,

"Is there yet a portion for us, and an inheritance in the house of our father?"

(15)

"Are we not regarded as foreigners by him, because he has sold us and completely consumed אֶת our money?"

(16)

"For all the wealth that הִצִּיל אֱלֹהִים (Elohim has taken away) from our father, it belongs to us and to our sons. So now, all that אָמַר אֱלֹהִים (Elohim said) to you, do."

Jacob Leaves Laban

(17) Then Ya-a-kov (*Jacob*) got up and put אֶת his children וְאֶת (*and **) his wives on the camels.

(18) And he drove אֵת all his livestock וְאֶת (*and **) all his possessions that he had acquired, the livestock of his possession that he had acquired in Pad-de-nah~A-ram, in order to go to Yitz-khak (*Isaac*) his father, to the land of K'na-an.

(19) Now La-van had gone to shear אֶת his sheep, and Ra-khel stole אֶת the household idols that belonged to her father.

(20) And Ya-a-kov (*Jacob*) deceived אֵת the heart of La-van the A-ra-mi (*Aramean*) by not telling him that he intended to flee.

(21) Then he fled with all that he had, and arose and crossed אֶת the stream and set אֶת his face toward the mountain of the Gil-ad.

Laban Pursues Jacob

(22) And on the third day it was told to La-van that Ya-a-kov (*Jacob*) had fled.

(23) Then he took אֶת his brothers with him and pursued after him, a seven-day journey, and he followed אֹתוֹ (* *him*) on the mountain of the Gil-ad.

(24) וַיָּבֹא אֱלֹהִים (*And Elohim came*) to La-van the A-ra-mi (*Aramean*) in a dream at night וַיֹּאמֶר (*and He said*) to him,

הִשָּׁמֶר לְךָ פֶּן-תְּדַבֵּר

עִם-יַעֲקֹב

מִטּוֹב עַד-רָע

Beware for you lest you speak

with Jacob,

from good unto evil.

(25) And La-van overtook אֶת Ya-a-kov (*Jacob*). Now Ya-a-kov (*Jacob*) had pitched אֶת his tent in the mountain, and La-van pitched with אֶת his brothers in the mountain of the Gil-ad.

(26) Then La-van said to Ya-a-kov (*Jacob*),

Level One   בְּרֵאשִׁית ~ לא

"What have you done and deceived אֶת my heart and have lead away אֶת my daughters like captives of the sword?"

(27)

"Why did you hide your intention to flee and trick אֹתִי (* me), and did not tell me so that I would have sent you away with joy and song and tambourine and lyre?"

(28)

"And why did you not give me opportunity to kiss my grandsons and my daughters goodbye? Now you have behaved foolishly by doing this."

(29)

"My hand is לְאֵל (to El) to do with you רָע (evil) וֵאלֹהֵי אֲבִיכֶם (and the Elohim of your father) אָמַר (He spoke) to me last night saying,

הִשָּׁמֶר לְךָ מִדַּבֵּר

עִם-יַעֲקֹב

מִטּוֹב עַד-רָע

Beware for you from speaking

with Jacob,

from good unto evil.

(30)

"Now, you have surely gone because you desperately longed for the house of your father, but why did you steal אֶת אֱלֹהָי (my elohim)?"

(31) Then Ya-a-kov (Jacob) answered and said to La-van,

> "Because I was afraid, for I said,
>
> > 'Lest you take אֵת your daughters from me by force.' "

(32)

> "But with whomever you find אֶת- אֱלֹהֶיךָ (* your elohim), he shall not live. In the presence of our brothers now identify what is with me that is yours and take it."

Now Ya-a-kov (*Jacob*) did not know that Ra-khel had stolen them.

Laban Searches for His Idols

(33) Then La-van went into the tent of Ya-a-kov (Jacob) and the tent of Le-ah and the tent of the two female servants and he found nothing. And he came out of the tent of Le-ah and went into the tent of Ra-khel.

(34) Now Ra-khel had taken אֵת the household idols and put them in the saddle bag of the camel and sat on them. And La-van searched אֵת the whole tent thoroughly but did not find them.

(35) And she said to her father,

> "Let there not be anger in the eyes of אֲדֹנִי (my lord), for I am not able to rise before you, for the way of women is with me."

And he searched carefully and did not find אֵת the household idols.

(36) Then Ya-a-kov (*Jacob*) became angry and quarreled with La-van. Ya-a-kov (*Jacob*) answered and said to La-van,

Level One   בְּרֵאשִׁית ~ לֹא

(37)   "What is my offense? What is my sin that you pursued after me?"

"For you have searched אֶת all my vessels and what did you find from all the vessels of your house? Set it before my brothers and your brothers that they may judge between the two of us!"

(38)   "These twenty years I was with you; your ewes and your female goats did not miscarry, and the rams of your flocks I did not eat."

(39)   "I brought no mangled carcass to you -- I bore its loss. From my hand you sought it, whether stolen by day or stolen by night."

(40)   "There I was, during the day the heat consumed me, and the cold by night, and my sleep fled from my eyes."

(41)   "These twenty years I have been in your house. I served you fourteen years for your two daughters and six years for your flock, and you have changed אֶת my wages ten times."

(42)   "Except אֱלֹהֵי אָבִי (the Elohim of my father) אֱלֹהֵי אַבְרָהָם (the Elohim of Abraaham) and the dread of Yitz-khak (Isaac) had not been for me, indeed now you would have sent me away empty-handed. רָאָה אֱלֹהִים (Elohim saw) אֶת my humiliation וְאֶת (and *) the weariness of my palms וַיּוֹכַח (and He corrected) last night."

185

(43) Then La-van answered and said to Ya-a-kov (*Jacob*),

> "The daughters are my daughters and the grandsons are my grandsons, and the flocks are my flocks, and all that אַתָּה (*you*) see, it is mine. Now, what can I do for these my daughters today, or for their children whom they have borne?"

A Covenant Between Jacob and Laban

(44)
> "So now, come, let us make a covenant, me וְאַתָּה (*and you*), and let it be a witness between me and you."

(45) And Ya-a-kov (*Jacob*) took a stone and set it up as a monument.

(46) And Ya-a-kov (*Jacob*) said to his brothers,

> "Gather stones."

And they took stones and made a pile of stones, and they ate there on the mound.

(47) And La-van called it Y'gar~Sa-ha-du-ta, but Ya-a-kov (*Jacob*) called it Gal-ed.

(48) Then La-van said,

> "This הַגַּל (*mound*) is עֵד (*a witness*) between me and you today."

Therefore, its name is called גַּלְעֵד (*Galeed*).

(49) וְהַמִּצְפָּה (*and the Mizpah*) which he said,

> יִצֶף יהוה (*YHVH watch*) between me and you because we are concealed one from another."

Level One   בְּרֵאשִׁית ~ לֹא

(50)

"If you humiliate אֶת *my daughters, and if you take wives over my daughters, when there is no man with us, see,* אֱלֹהִים *(Elohim) is a witness between me and you."*

(51) And La-van said to Ya-a-kov (*Jacob*),

"See, this mound, and see the monument that I have set up between me and you."

(52)

"This mound is a witness, and the monument is a witness, that I will not pass beyond אֶת *this mound to you, and that* אַתָּה *(you) will not pass beyond* אֶת *this mound* וְאֶת *(and *) this monument to me* לְרָעָה *(for evil)."*

(53)

אֱלֹהֵי אַבְרָהָם *(the Elohim of Av-ra-ham)* וֵאלֹהֵי נָחוֹר *(and the Elohim of Na-khor)* אֱלֹהֵי אֲבִיהֶם *(the Elohim of)their father) judge between us."*

Then Ya-a-kov (*Jacob*) swore by the dread of his father Yitz-khak (*Isaac*).

(54) And Ya-a-kov (*Jacob*) offered a sacrifice on the mountain, and he called his brothers to eat bread. And they ate bread and spent the night on the mountain.

(55) (32:1) And La-van arose early in the morning and kissed his grandsons and his daughters, and blessed אֶתְהֶם (* *them*). Then La-van departed and returned to his homeland.

Chapter 32

The Camp Of Elohim

(1) (32:2) And Ya-a-kov (*Jacob*) went on his way, and מַלְאֲכֵי אֱלֹהִים (*messengers of Elohim*) met him.

(2) (32:3) And when he saw them, Ya-a-kov (*Jacob*) said,

"This is מַחֲנֵה אֱלֹהִים (*the camp of Elohim*)."

And he called the name of that place מַחֲנָיִם (*Mahanaim*).

Jacob Sends Messengers To Esau

(3) (32:4) Then Ya-a-kov (*Jacob*) sent מַלְאָכִים (*messengers*) before him to E-sav his brother, to the land of Se-ir, the field of E-dom.

(4) (32:5) And he instructed אֹתָם (** them*), saying,

"Thus you must say לַאדֹנִי (*to my lord*), to E-sav,

'Thus says your servant Ya-a-kov (*Jacob*), I have sojourned with La-van, and I have remained there until now.'

(5) (32:6)

'And I have acquired cattle, male donkeys, flocks, and male and female servants, and I have sent to declare לַאדֹנִי (*to my lord*), to find favor in your eyes.' "

(6) (32:7) And הַמַּלְאָכִים (*the messengers*) returned to Ya-a-kov (*Jacob*) and said,

Level One

בְּרֵאשִׁית ~ לב

> "We came to your brother, to E-sav, and he is coming to meet you, and four hundred men are with him."

(7) (32:8) Then Ya-a-kov (*Jacob*) was very frightened and distressed. So he divided אֶת the people that were with אִתּוֹ (** him*) וְאֶת (*and **) the flock וְאֶת (*and **) the herd, and the camels into two camps.

(8) (32:9) And he said,

> "If E-sav comes to one camp and destroys it, the remaining camp will be able to escape."

Jacob Prays

(9) (32:10) Then Ya-a-kov (*Jacob*) said,

> וֵאלֹהֵי (*the Elohim of my father Av-ra-ham*) אֱלֹהֵי **אָבִי אַבְרָהָם**
> יהוה (*and the Elohim of my father Yitz-khak/Isaac*) **אָבִי יִצְחָק**
> הָאֹמֵר (*YHVH the One Who said*) to me,
>
> שׁוּב לְאַרְצְךָ
> וּלְמוֹלַדְתֶּךָ
> וְאֵיטִיבָה עִמָּךְ
>
> *Return to your land*
> *and to your kindred,*
> *and I will deal well with you.*

(10) (32:11)
> "I am not worthy of all the kindness and all the faithfulness that

Genesis ~ 32

You have shown אֶת Your servant, for with only my staff I crossed this אֶת the Yar-den (Jordan), and now I have become two camps."

(11) (32:12)

"Please rescue me from the hand of my brother, from the hand of E-sav, for I fear אֹתוֹ (* him), lest he come and attack me, mother with children."

(12) (32:13)

וְאַתָּה אָמַרְתָּ (And You Yourself said)

הֵיטֵב אֵיטִיב עִמָּךְ

וְשַׂמְתִּי אֶת־זַרְעֲךָ

כְּחוֹל הַיָּם

אֲשֶׁר לֹא־יִסָּפֵר מֵרֹב

I will surely deal well with you
and make * your seed
like the sand of the sea
that it cannot be numbered from multitude.

Gifts For Esau

(13) (32:14) And he lodged there that night. Then he took from what he had with him a gift for E-sav his brother:

(14) (32:15) two hundred female goats, twenty male goats, two hundred ewes, twenty rams,

(15) (32:16) thirty milk camels with their young, forty cows, ten bulls, twenty female donkeys, and ten male donkeys.

Level One   בְּרֵאשִׁית ~ לב

(16) (32:17) And he put them in the hand of his servants, herd by herd, and said to his servants,

> "Cross on ahead before me וְרֶוַח (and an interval) you shall put between herds."

(17) (32:18) And he instructed אֶת the first, saying,

> "When E-sav my brother comes upon you and asks you, saying,
>
>> 'Whose are אַתָּה (you) and where are you going? To whom do these animals ahead of you belong?'"

(18) (32:19)

> "Then you must say,
>
>> 'To your servant, to Ya-a-kov (Jacob). It is a gift sent לַאדֹנִי (to my lord), to E-sav. Now behold, he is also coming after us.'"

(19) (32:20) And he also instructed אֶת the second servant and also אֶת the third, and also אֶת all the ones going after the herds, saying,

> "You must speak to E-sav according to this word when you find אֹתוֹ (* him)."

(20) (32:21)

> "And moreover, you shall say,
>
>> 'Look, your servant Ya-a-kov (Jacob) is behind us.'"

For he thought,

> "Let me appease him with the gift going before me, and afterward

Genesis ~ 32

I will see his face. Perhaps he will show me favor."

(21) (32:22) So the gift passed on before him, but he himself spent that night in the camp.

(22) (32:23) That night he arose and took אֶת his two wives וְאֶת (*and* *) his two female servants וְאֶת (*and* *) his eleven children and crossed אֶת the ford of Ya-bok.

(23) (32:24) And he took them and sent them across אֶת the stream. Then he sent across אֶת all his possessions.

Jacob Wrestles

(24) (32:25) And Ya-a-kov (*Jacob*) remained alone, and a Man wrestled with him until the breaking of the dawn.

(25) (32:26) And when He saw that He could not prevail against him, He struck his hip socket, so that Ya-a-kov's (*Jacob*) hip socket was sprained as He wrestled with him.

(26) (32:27) וַיֹּאמֶר (*And He said*)

Send Me,
for dawn is breaking.

But he answered,

"I will not send you unless You bless me.

Level One   בְּרֵאשִׁית ~ לב

Jacob To Israel

(27) (32:28) וַיֹּאמֶר (*And He said*) to him,

מַה־שְּׁמֶךָ

What is your name?

And he said,

"*Ya-a-kov (Jacob).*"

(28) (32:29) וַיֹּאמֶר (*And He said*)

לֹא יַעֲקֹב יֵאָמֵר עוֹד שִׁמְךָ

כִּי אִם־יִשְׂרָאֵל

כִּי־שָׂרִיתָ עִם־אֱלֹהִים

וְעִם־אֲנָשִׁים

וַתּוּכָל

Your name shall no longer be said Jacob,
but rather Israel,
because you have persevered with Elohim
and with men
and have overcome.

(29) (32:30) Then Ya-a-kov (*Jacob*) asked and said,

"*Please tell me Your name.*"

וַיֹּאמֶר (*And He said*)

Genesis ~ 32

לָמָּה זֶּה תִּשְׁאַל לִשְׁמִי

Why do you ask this for My name?

וַיְבָרֶךְ (*And He blessed*) אֹתוֹ (* *him*) there.

(30) (32:31) Then Ya-a-kov (*Jacob*) called the name of the place פְּנִיאֵל (*Peniel*)

"For I have seen אֱלֹהִים (*Elohim*) פָּנִים אֶל־פָּנִים (*face to face*) and my soul is rescued."

(31) (32:32) Then the sun rose upon him as he passed אֶת P'nu-el, and he was limping because of his hip.

(32) (32:33) Therefore, the sons of Yis-ra-el do not eat אֶת the sinew of the failed nerve that is on the socket of the hip unto this day, because נָגַע (*He touched*) the socket of the thigh of Ya-a-kov (*Jacob*) at the sinew of the failed nerve.

Chapter 33

Jacob Meets With Esau

(1) And Ya-a-kov (*Jacob*) lifted up his eyes and looked. And behold, E-sav was coming and four hundred men were with him. And he divided אֶת the children among Le-ah and among Ra-khel, and among the two of his female servants.

(2) And he put אֶת the female servants וְאֶת (*and* *) their children first וְאֶת (*and* *) Le-ah and her children next וְאֶת (*and* *) Ra-khel וְאֶת (*and* *) Yo-sef last.

(3) And he himself passed on before them and bowed down to the ground seven times until he came to his brother.

(4) But E-sav ran to meet him, and embraced him, and fell upon his neck and kissed him, and they wept.

(5) Then E-sav lifted up אֶת his eyes and saw אֶת the women וְאֶת (*and* *) the children and said,

> *"Who are these with you?"*

And he said,

> *"The children whom* חָנַן אֱלֹהִים *(Elohim has graciously given)* אֶת *your servant."*

(6) Then the female servants drew near, they and their children, and they bowed down.

(7) Then Le-ah and her children drew near and bowed down, and afterward Yo-sef and Ra-khel drew near and they bowed down.

(8) And he said,

> *"What do you mean by all this company that I have met?"*

Genesis ~ 33

Then he said,

> "To find favor in the eyes of אֲדֹנִי (my lord)."

(9) Then E-sav said,

> "I have enough my brother; keep what you have."

(10) And Ya-a-kov (*Jacob*) said,

> "No, please, if I have found favor in your eyes, you must take my gift from my hand, for then I have seen your face which is like seeing the face of אֱלֹהִים (Elohim) and you have received me."

(11)

> "Please take אֵת my blessing which has been brought to you, for חַנַּנִי אֱלֹהִים (Elohim has dealt graciously with me), and because I have enough."

And he urged him, so he took it.

(12) Then he said,

> "Let us journey and go on, and I will go ahead of you."

(13) But he said to him,

> אֲדֹנִי (*My lord*) knows that the children are frail, and the flocks and the cattle which are nursing are a concern to me. Now if they drove them hard for a day all the flocks would die."

(14)

> "Let אֲדֹנִי (my lord) pass on before his servant and I will move along slowly at the pace of the livestock that are ahead of me, and at the pace of the children until I come to אֲדֹנִי (my lord) in Se-ir."

Level One   בְּרֵאשִׁית ~ לג

(15) And E-sav said,

> "Please, I shall leave with you some from the people who are with אִתִּי (*me)."

But he said,

> "What need is there? Let me find favor in the eyes of אֲדֹנִי (my lord)."

(16) So E-sav turned that day on his way to Se-ir.

Jacob Settles In Shechem

(17) But Ya-a-kov (*Jacob*) traveled toward Su-kot, and he built for himself a house, and he made סֻכֹּת (*shelters*) for his livestock. Therefore, he called the name of the place סֻכּוֹת (*Succoth*).

(18) And Ya-a-kov (*Jacob*) came safely to the city of Sh'khem which is in the land of K'na-an, on his way from Pad-de-nah~A-ram. And he camped אֶת before the city.

(19) And he bought אֶת a portion of the field where he pitched his tent for one hundred pieces of money from the hand of the sons of Kha-mor, father of Sh'khem.

(20) And there he erected an altar and called it אֵל אֱלֹהֵי יִשְׂרָאֵל (El, the Elohim of Yis-ra-el).

Chapter 34

Dinah Is Defiled

(1) Now Di-nah the daughter of Le-ah, whom she had borne to Ya-a-kov (Jacob), went out to see the daughters of the land.

(2) And Sh'khem, the son of Kha-mor the Khi-vi (*Hivite*), the prince of the land, saw אֹתָהּ (** her*). And he took אֹתָהּ (** her*) and lay with אֹתָהּ (** her*) and humbled her.

(3) And his soul clung to Di-nah, the daughter of Ya-a-kov (*Jacob*), and he loved אֶת the young woman and spoke to the heart of the young woman.

(4) And Sh'khem said to Kha-mor his father, saying,

"Take for me אֶת this girl for a wife."

(5) And Ya-a-kov (Jacob) heard that he defiled אֶת Di-nah his daughter, and his sons were with אֶת his flocks in the field. And Ya-a-kov (*Jacob*) kept silent until they came.

Shechem Meets Jacob

(6) And Kha-mor, father of Sh'khem, went out to Ya-a-kov (*Jacob*) to speak with אֹתוֹ (** him*).

(7) And the sons of Ya-a-kov (*Jacob*) came in from the field when they heard it. And the men were distressed and very angry because he had done a disgraceful thing in Yis-ra-el by lying with אֶת the daughter of Ya-a-kov (Jacob) -- something that should not be done.

(8) And Kha-mor spoke with אֹתָם (** them*) saying,

"Sh'khem my son is in love with your daughter. Please give אֹתָהּ (*

Level One   בְּרֵאשִׁית ~ לד

her) to him for a wife."

(9)

"Make marriages with אִתָּנוּ (* us). Give us your daughters וְאֶת (and *) our daughters you shall take for yourselves."

(10)

"You shall dwell with אֶת us and the land shall be before you; settle and trade in it, and acquire property in it."

(11) Then Sh'khem said to her father and to her brothers,

"Let me find favor in your eyes, and whatever you say to me I will give."

(12)

"Make the bride price and gift as high as you like; I will give what you say to me. But give me אֶת the young woman for a wife."

(13) Then the sons of Ya-a-kov (Jacob) answered אֶת Sh'khem וְאֶת (and *) Kha-mor his father speaking deceitfully, because he had defiled אֶת Di-nah their sister.

(14) And they said to them,

"We cannot do this thing, to give אֶת our sister to a man who has foreskin, for that is a disgrace for us."

(15)

"Only on this condition will we give consent to you; if you will become like us -- every male among you to be circumcised."

(16)

"And we will give אֶת our daughters to you וְאֶת (and *) your daughters we will take for ourselves and we will dwell with אִתְּכֶם (* you) and become one people."

(17)

"But if you will not listen to us, to be circumcised, then we will take אֶת our daughters and we will go."

(18) And their words were good in the eyes of Kha-mor and in the eyes of Sh'khem, the son of Kha-mor.

(19) And the young man did not delay to do the thing, for he wanted the daughter of Ya-a-kov (*Jacob*). Now he was the most honored of his father's house.

Circumcision Of Shechem

(20) Then Kha-mor and his son Sh'khem came to the gate of their city, and they spoke to the men of their city, saying,

(21)

"These men are at peace with אִתָּנוּ (* us). Let them dwell in the land and let them trade in אֹתָהּ (* it). And, behold, the land is wide on both hands before them. Let us take אֶת their daughters as wives, and וְאֶת (and *) let us give our daughters to them."

(22)

"Only on this condition will they give consent to us, to live with אִתָּנוּ (* us) and to become one people -- when every male among us is circumcised as they are circumcised."

(23)

"Will not their livestock and their property and all their animals be ours? Only let us give consent to them so they will live with אִתָּנוּ

Level One　　　　　　　　　　　　　　　　　　　　　　　　　בְּרֵאשִׁית ~ לד

(* us)."

(24) And all those who went out of the gate of his city listened to Kha-mor and to Sh'khem his son and they were circumcised -- Every male of all those who went out of the gate of his city.

Overthrow Of Shechem

(25) And it happened that on the third day, while they were in pain, two of the sons of Ya-a-kov (*Jacob*), Shim-on and Le-vi, the brothers of Di-nah, each took his sword and came against the unsuspecting city and killed all the males.

(26) וְאֶת (*and* *) Kha-mor וְאֶת (*and* *) Sh'khem his son, they killed with the edge of a sword, and they took אֶת Di-nah from the house of Sh'khem and went out.

(27) The other sons of Ya-a-kov (*Jacob*) came upon the slain and plundered the city, because they had defiled their sister.

(28) אֶת their flock וְאֶת (*and* *) their herd וְאֶת (*and* *) their donkeys וְאֶת (*and* *) whatever was in the city וְאֶת (*and* *) whatever was in the field -- they took.

(29) וְאֶת (*and* *) all their wealth וְאֶת (*and* *) all their little ones וְאֶת (*and* *) their women -- they captured and plundered וְאֶת (*and* *) all that was in the house.

(30) Then Ya-a-kov (*Jacob*) said to Shim-on and Le-vi,

> "You have troubled אֹתִי (* *me*), making me stink among the inhabitants of the land, among the K'na-a-ni (*Canaanite*) and the P'ri-zi (*Perizzite*)! I am few in number! If they gather against me and attack me, I will be destroyed -- I and my household!"

(31) But they said,

> "Shall he treat אֶת our sister like a prostitute?"

Chapter 35

Jacob Goes To Bet-El

(1) וַיֹּאמֶר אֱלֹהִים (*And Elohim said*) to Ya-a-kov (*Jacob*),

קוּם עֲלֵה בֵית-אֵל

וְשֶׁב-שָׁם

וַעֲשֵׂה-שָׁם מִזְבֵּחַ

לָאֵל הַנִּרְאֶה אֵלֶיךָ

בְּבָרְחֲךָ מִפְּנֵי

עֵשָׂו אָחִיךָ

Arise, go up to Bet-El / the house of El
and dwell there,
and make there an altar
to El, the One Who appeared to you
in your fleeing from the face of
Esau your brother.

(2) Then Ya-a-kov (*Jacob*) said to his household and to all who were with him,

"Get rid of אֶת-אֱלֹהֵי הַנֵּכָר (* *the elohim of the foreigner*) that are in your midst and purify yourselves and change your garments."

(3)

"Then let us make ready and let us go up to בֵּית-אֵל (*Bet-El / the house of El*), so that I can make an altar there לָאֵל (*to El*) Who

Level One בְּרֵאשִׁית ~ לה

answered אֹתִי (* me) in the day of my trouble, and Who has been with me in the way that I have gone."

(4) So they gave to Ya-a-kov (Jacob) אֵת כָּל-אֱלֹהֵי הַנֵּכָר (* all the elohim of the foreigner) that were in their hands וְאֶת (and *) the pendants that were in their ears. And Ya-a-kov (Jacob) buried אֹתָם (* them) under the terebinth which was near Sh'khem.

(5) Then they set out on their journey, and the terror of אֱלֹהִים (Elohim) was upon the cities that were all around them, so that they did not pursue after the sons of Ya-a-kov (Jacob).

(6) And Ya-a-kov (Jacob) came to Luz which was in the land of K'na-an -- that is בֵּית-אֵל (Bet-El / the house of El), he and all the people that were with him.

(7) And he built an altar there and called the place אֵל בֵּית-אֵל (El of Bet-El / the house of El), for there נִגְלוּ הָאֱלֹהִים (the Elohim were revealed) to him when he fled before his brother.

(8) And D'vo-rah, the nurse of Riv-kah (Rebekah), died. And she was buried below בֵּית-אֵל (Bet-El / the house of El), under the oak. And its name was called Al-lon~Ba-khut.

Jacob To Israel Confirmed

(9) וַיֵּרָא אֱלֹהִים (And Elohim appeared) to Ya-a-kov (Jacob) again when he came from Pad-de-nah~A-ram וַיְבָרֶךְ אֹתוֹ (and He blessed * him).

(10) וַיֹּאמֶר אֱלֹהִים (And Elohim said) to him,

שִׁמְךָ יַעֲקֹב
לֹא-יִקָּרֵא שִׁמְךָ עוֹד יַעֲקֹב

Genesis ~ 35

Your name is Jacob.
Your name shall no longer be called Jacob,

כִּי אִם-יִשְׂרָאֵל

יִהְיֶה שְׁמֶךָ

but rather Israel
shall be your name.

וַיִּקְרָא (*And He called*) אֶת his name Yis-ra-el.
(11) וַיֹּאמֶר אֱלֹהִים (*And Elohim said*) to him,

אֲנִי אֵל שַׁדַּי

פְּרֵה וּרְבֵה

גּוֹי וּקְהַל גּוֹיִם

יִהְיֶה מִמֶּךָּ

וּמְלָכִים מֵחֲלָצֶיךָ

יֵצֵאוּ

I am El Almighty.
Be fruitful and increase.
A nation and an assembly of nations
shall be from you,
and kings from your loins
shall come forth.

(12)

וְאֶת-הָאָרֶץ אֲשֶׁר נָתַתִּי

Level One   בְּרֵאשִׁית ~ לה

לְאַבְרָהָם וּלְיִצְחָק

לְךָ אֶתְּנֶנָּה

And * the land that I gave

to Av-ra-ham and to Yitz-khak (Isaac),

to you, I am giving it.

וּלְזַרְעֲךָ אַחֲרֶיךָ

אֶתֵּן אֶת-הָאָרֶץ

And to your seed after you

I am giving * the land.

(13) וַיַּעַל אֱלֹהִים (*And Elohim ascended*) from on him at the place where דִּבֶּר אִתּוֹ (*He spoke with * him*).

(14) And Ya-a-kov (*Jacob*) set up a pillar at the place where דִּבֶּר אִתּוֹ (*He spoke with * him*), a pillar of stone. And he poured out a drink offering upon it, and poured oil on it.

(15) And Ya-a-kov (*Jacob*) called אֵת the name of the place where דִּבֶּר אִתּוֹ (*He spoke with * him*) בֵּית-אֵל (*Bet-El / the house of El*).

Death Of Rachel

(16) Then they journeyed from בֵּית-אֵל (*Bet-El / the house of El*). And when they were still some distance to come to the land of Ef-ra-ta, Ra-khel went into labor. And she had hard labor.

(17) And when her labor was the most difficult the midwife said to her,

Genesis ~ 35

"Do not be afraid for you have another son."

(18) And it happened that when her life was departing, for she was dying, she called his name Ben~O-ni. But his father called him בִּנְיָמִין (*Benjamin*).

(19) And Ra-khel died and she was buried on the way to Ef-ra-ta -- that is, Bet~Le-khem.

(20) And Ya-a-kov (*Jacob*) erected a pillar at her burial site. That is the pillar of the burial site of Ra-khel unto this day.

(21) And Yis-ra-el journeyed on and pitched his tent beyond the tower of E-der.

(22) And while Yis-ra-el was living in that land R'u-ven went and had sexual relations with אֵת Bil-hah, his father's concubine. And Yis-ra-el heard about it.

Sons Of Jacob

Now the sons of Ya-a-kov (*Jacob*) were twelve.

(23) The sons of Le-ah: The firstborn of Ya-a-kov (*Jacob*) was R'u-ven. Then Shim-on, Le-vi, Y'hu-dah, Yis-sas-khar, and Z'vu-lun.

(24) The sons of Ra-khel: Yo-sef and Ben-ya-min.

(25) The sons of Bil-hah, the female servant of Ra-khel: Dan and Naf-ta-li.

(26) The sons of Zil-pah, the female servant of Le-ah: Gad and A-sher. These were the sons of Ya-a-kov (*Jacob*) who were born to him in Pad-de-nah~A-ram.

Death Of Isaac

(27) And Ya-a-kov (*Jacob*) came to Yitz-khak (*Isaac*) his father at Mam-re at Kir-yat~Ha-Ar-ba -- that is, Hev-ron, where Av-ra-ham and Yitz-khak (*Isaac*) sojourned.

(28) Now the days of Yitz-khak (*Isaac*) were a hundred and eighty years.

(29) And Yitz-khak (*Isaac*) passed away and died, and was gathered to his people, old and full of days. And his sons E-sav and Ya-a-kov (*Jacob*) buried אֹתוֹ (* *him*).

Chapter 36

Descendants Of Esau

(1) Now these are the descendants of E-sav -- he is E-dom.

(2-3) E-sav took אֵת his wives from the daughters of K'na-an: אֶת A-dah, daughter of Ay-lon, the Khit-ti (*Hittite*) וְאֶת (*and* *) A-ho-li-va-mah, daughter of A-nah, the daughter of Ziv-on, the Khi-vi (*Hivite*) וְאֶת (*and* *) Bas-mat, the daughter of Yish-ma-el, the sister of N'va-yot.

(4) And A-dah bore to E-sav אֶת E-li-faz; and Bas-mat bore אֶת R'u-el;

(5) and A-ho-li-va-mah bore אֵת Y'ush וְאֶת (*and* *) Ya-lam וְאֶת (*and* *) Ko-rakh. These are the sons of E-sav who were born to him in the land of K'na-an.

Esau Leaves Jacob

(6) And E-sav took אֵת his wives וְאֶת (*and* *) his sons וְאֶת (*and* *) his daughters וְאֶת (*and* *) all the persons of his household וְאֶת (*and* *) his cattle וְאֶת (*and* *) all his animals וְאֵת (*and* *) all his goods that he had acquired in the land of K'na-an, and went to a land away from the face of his brother Ya-a-kov (*Jacob*).

(7) For their possessions were too many to live together, so that the land of their sojourning was not able to support אֹתָם (* *them*) on account of their livestock.

(8) So E-sav dwelled in the mountain of Se-ir -- E-sav, he is E-dom.

Descendants Of Esau - More Detail

Genesis ~ 36

(9) Now these are the descendants of E-sav, the father of E-dom, in the mountain of Se-ir.

(10) These are the names of the sons of E-sav: E-li-faz, the son of A-dah, the wife of E-sav; R'u-el, the son of Bas-mat, the wife of E-sav.

(11) The sons of E-li-faz were Tay-man, O-mar, Tz'fo, and Ga-tam, and K'naz.

(12) And Tim-na was the concubine of E-li-faz, the son of E-sav. And she bore אֶת A-ma-lek to E-li-faz. These are the sons of A-dah, the wife of E-sav.

(13) Now these are the sons of R'u-el: Na-khat and Ze-rakh, Sham-mah, and Miz-zah. These are the sons of Bas-mat, the wife of E-sav.

(14) Now these are the sons of A-ho-li-va-mah, the daughter of A-nah, daughter of Ziv-on, the wife of E-sav: She bore to E-sav אֶת Y'ush וְאֶת (*and* *) Ya-lam וְאֶת (*and* *) Ko-rakh.

Chiefs Of Esau

(15) These are the chiefs of the sons of E-sav. The sons of E-li-faz, the firstborn of E-sav: Chief Tay-man, Chief O-mar, Chief Z'fo, Chief K'naz,

(16) Chief Ko-rakh, Chief Ga-tam, Chief A-ma-lek. These are the chiefs of E-li-faz in the land of E-dom. These are the sons of A-dah.

(17) Now these are the sons R'u-el, the son of E-sav: Chief Na-khat, Chief Ze-rakh, Chief Sham-mah, Chief Miz-zah. These are the chiefs of R'u-el in the land of E-dom. These are the sons of Bas-mat, the wife of E-sav.

(18) Now these are the sons of A-ho-li-va-mah, the wife of E-sav: Chief Y'ush, Chief Ja-lam, Chief Ko-rakh. These are the chiefs born of A-ho-li-va-mah, the daughter of A-nah, the wife of E-sav.

(19) These are the sons of E-sav, and these are their chiefs (he is E-dom).

Level One   בְּרֵאשִׁית ~ לו

Sons Of Seir

(20-21) These are the sons of Se-ir, the Kho-ri (*Horite*), the inhabitants of the land: Lo-tan and Sho-val and Tziv-on and A-nah, and Di-shon and Ay-tzer and Di-shan. These are the chiefs of the Kho-ri (*Horite*), the sons of Se-ir in the land of E-dom.

(22) And the sons of Lo-tan were Kho-ri and He-mam. And the sister of Lo-tan was Tim-na.

(23) Now these are the sons of Sho-val: Al-van and Ma-na-khat and Ay-val, Sh'fo and O-nam.

(24) Now these are the sons of Tziv-on: both Ai-yah and A-nah -- he is A-nah who found אֶת the hot springs in the wilderness בִּרְעֹתוֹ (in his shepherding) אֶת the donkeys of Tziv-on his father.

(25) Now these are the sons of A-nah: Di-shon and A-ho-li-va-mah, the daughter of A-nah.

(26) Now these are the sons of Di-shon: Khem-dan and Esh-ban and Yit-ran and Kh'ran.

(27) These are the sons of E-tzer: Bil-han and Za-a-van and A-kan.

(28) These are the sons of Di-shan: Uz and A-ran.

Chiefs Of The Horite

(29-30) These are the chiefs of the Kho-ri (*Horite*): Chief Lo-tan, Chief Sho-val, Chief Ziv-on, Chief A-nah, Chief Di-shon, Chief Ay-tzer, Chief Di-shan. These are the chiefs of the Kho-ri (*Horite*), according to their chiefs in the land of Se-ir.

Kings Of Edom

(31) Now these are the kings who reigned in the land of E-dom before any king ruled over the sons of Yis-ra-el.

(32) Be-la the son of B'or reigned in E-dom. And the name of his city was Din-ha-vah.

(33) And Be-la died, and Yo-vav, the son of Ze-rakh from Batz-rah, reigned in his place.

(34) And Yo-vav died, and Khu-sham from the land of the Tay-ma-ni (Temanite) reigned in his place.

(35) And Khu-sham died, and Ha-dad, son of B'dad, who defeated אֶת Mid-yan in the field of Mo-av reigned in his place. And the name of his city was A-vit.

(36) And Ha-dad died, and Sam-lah from Mas-re-kah reigned in his place.

(37) And Sam-lah died, and Sha-ul from R'kho-vot on the river reigned in his place.

(38) And Sha-ul died, and Ba-al~Kha-nan, the son of Akh-bor, reigned in his place.

(39) And Ba-al~Kha-nan the son of Akh-bor died, and Ha-dar reigned in his place. And the name of his city was Pa-u, and the name of his wife was M'hay-tav-el, the daughter of Mat-red, daughter of May~Za-hav.

(40) Now these are the names of the chiefs of E-sav according to their families, according to their dwelling places, by their names: Chief Tim-na, Chief Al-vah, Chief Y'tet,

(41) Chief A-ho-li-va-mah, Chief E-lah, Chief Pi-non,

(42) Chief K'naz, Chief Tay-man, Chief Miv-tzar,

(43) Chief Mag-di-el, Chief I-ram.

These are the chiefs of E-dom according to their settlements in the land of their possession. E-sav, he is the father of E-dom.

Chapter 37

Joseph's Coat

(1) And Ya-a-kov (*Jacob*) settled in the land of the sojourning of his father, in the land of K'na-an.

(2) These are the generations of Ya-a-kov (*Jacob*). Yo-sef, being seventeen years old, was רֹעֶה (*shepherding*) the flock with אֶת his brothers. Now he was a young man with אֶת the sons of Bil-hah וְאֶת (*and **) the sons of Zil-pah, the wives of his father. And Yo-sef brought אֶת their רָעָה (*evil*) whisperings to his father.

(3) Now Yis-ra-el loved אֶת Yo-sef more than all his sons, for he was a son of his old age. And he made for him a long garment.

(4) When his brothers saw that their father loved אֹתוֹ (** him*) more than all his brothers, they hated אֹתוֹ (** him*) and were not able to speak to him לְשָׁלֹם (*for peace*).

Joseph's Dreams

(5) And Yo-sef dreamed a dream, and he told it to his brothers. And they hated אֹתוֹ (** him*) even more.

(6) And he said to them,

> "Listen now to this dream that I dreamed."

(7)
> "Now behold, we were binding sheaves in the midst of the field and, behold, my sheaf stood up and it remained standing. Then behold, your sheaves gathered around and bowed down to my sheaf."

Genesis ~ 37

(8) Then his brothers said to him,

> "Will you really rule over us?"

And they hated אֹתוֹ (* *him*) even more on account of his dream and because of his words.

(9) Then he dreamed yet another dream and told אֹתוֹ (* *it*) to his brothers. And he said,

> "Behold, I dreamed a dream again, and behold, the sun and the moon and eleven stars were bowing down to me."

(10) And he told it to his father and to his brothers. And his father rebuked him and said to him,

> "What is this dream that you have dreamed? Will I and your mother and your brothers indeed come to bow down to the ground to you?"

(11) And his brothers were jealous of him, but his father kept אֶת the word.

Joseph Betrayed

(12) Now his brothers went to pasture אֶת the flock of their father in Sh'khem.

(13) And Yis-ra-el said to Yo-sef,

> "Are not your brothers רֹעִים (*pasturing*) in Sh'khem? Come, let me send you to them."

And he said,

> "Here I am."

(14) Then he said to him,

Level One   בְּרֵאשִׁית ~ לז

> "Please, go see אֶת-שְׁלוֹם (* the peace of) your brothers וְאֶת-שְׁלוֹם (and * the peace of) the flock, then return word to me."

And he sent him from the valley of Hev-ron, and he arrived at Sh'khem.

(15) And a man found him, and behold, he was wandering about in a field. And the man asked him,

> "What are you seeking?"

(16) And he said,

> "I am seeking אֵת my brothers. Tell me, please, where they are רֹעִים (pasturing)."

(17) And the man said,

> "They have moved on from here, for I heard them saying,
>
> 'Let us go toward Do-tan.' "

Then Yo-sef went after his brothers and found them in Do-tan.

(18) And they saw אֹתוֹ (* him) from a distance. And before he drew near to them, they conspired against אֹתוֹ (* him) to kill him.

(19) And each said to his brothers,

(20)

> "Look, this possessor of dreams is coming. Now then, come, let us kill him and throw him in one of the pits. Then we will say an רָעָה (evil) animal devoured him. Then we will see what his dreams become."

(21) And R'u-ven heard it and delivered him from their hand and said,

> "We must not take his life."

(22) And R'u-ven said to them,

> "You must not shed blood. Throw אֹתוֹ (* him) into this cistern that is in the wilderness, but do not lay a hand on him."

So that he might rescue אֹתוֹ (* him) from their hand to return him to his father.

(23) And it happened that as Yo-sef came to his brothers they stripped אֶת Yo-sef of אֶת his garment, אֶת the long garment that was on him.

(24) And they took him and threw אֹתוֹ (* him) into the cistern and the cistern was empty; there was no water in it.

(25) Then they sat down to eat bread. And they lifted up their eyes and looked, and behold, a caravan of Yish-m'e-lim (*Ishmaelites*) was coming from the Gil-ad. And their camels were carrying perfume and balm and spices doing down to Mitz-ra-yim (*Egypt*).

(26) Then Y'hu-dah said to his brothers,

> "What profit is there if we kill אֶת our brother and conceal אֶת his blood?"

(27)

> "Come, let us sell him to the Yish-m'e-lim (*Ishmaelites*), but our hand shall not be against him, for he is our brother, our own flesh."

And his brothers agreed.

(28) And Mid-ya-nim (*Midianite*) merchants passed by. And they drew up and brought up אֶת Yo-sef from the cistern, and they sold אֶת Yo-sef to the Yish-m'e-lim (*Ishmaelites*) for twenty pieces of silver. And they brought אֶת Yo-sef to Mitz-ra-yim (*Egypt*).

Level One   בְּרֵאשִׁית ~ לז

(29) Then R'u-ven returned to the pit and, behold, Yo-sef was not in the cistern. And he tore אֶת his garments.

(30) And he returned to his brothers and said,

> "The boy is not! And I, where can I go?"

Jacob Is Deceived By His Sons

(31) Then they took אֶת the garment of Yo-sef and slaughtered a he-goat, and dipped אֶת the garment in the blood.

(32) And they sent אֶת the long garment and they brought it to their father and said,

> "We found this; please examine it. Is it the robe of your son or not?"

(33) And he recognized it and said,

> "The garment of my son! An רָעָה (evil) animal has devoured him! Yo-sef is surely torn to pieces!"

(34) And Ya-a-kov (*Jacob*) tore his garments and put sackcloth on his waist and mourned for his son many days.

(35) And all his sons and daughters tried to console him, but he refused to be consoled and he said because,

> "I shall go down to Sh'ol to my son mourning."

And his father wept for אֹתוֹ (* *him*).

Joseph Sold To Potiphar

(36) And the M'da-nim (*Midianites*) sold אֹתוֹ (* *him*) in Mitz-ra-yim (*Egypt*)

to Po-ti-far, a eunuch of Far-oh, chief of the guards.

Chapter 38

Judah And Tamar

(1) And it happened that at that time Y'hu-dah went down מֵאֵת (*from **) his brothers and turned aside to an A-dul-la-mi (*Adullamite*) man, whose name was Hi-rah.

(2) And Y'hu-dah saw there the daughter of a C'na-a-ni (*Canaanite*) man there and his name was Shu-a. And he took her and went to her.

(3) And she conceived and bore a son, and he called אֵת his name Er.

(4) And she conceived again and bore a son, and she called אֵת his name O-nan.

(5) And once again she bore a son, and she called אֵת his name She-lah. And he was in Kh'ziv when she bore אֹתוֹ (** him*).

(6) And Y'hu-dah took a wife for Er his firstborn, and her name was Ta-mar.

(7) And Er, the firstborn of Y'hu-dah, was רַע (*evil*) in the eyes of יהוה (*YHVH*) וַיְמִתֵהוּ יהוה (*and YHVH killed him*).

(8) Then Y'hu-dah said to O-nan,

> *"Go in to the wife of your brother and perform the duty of a brother-in-law to אֹתָהּ (* her), and raise up seed for your brother."*

(9) But O-nan knew that the seed would not be for him, so when he went in to the wife of his brother he would waste it on the ground so as not to give seed to his brother.

(10) וַיֵּרַע (*And he was evil*) in the sight of יהוה (*YHVH*) וַיָּמֶת (*and He killed*) אֹתוֹ (** him*) also.

(11) Then Y'hu-dah said to Ta-mar, his daughter-in-law,

Level One   בְּרֵאשִׁית ~ לח

> "Stay a widow in your father's house until She-lah my son grows up,"

for he feared he would also die like his brothers. So Ta-mar went and stayed in the house of her father.

(12) And in the course of time the daughter of Shu-a, the wife of Y'hu-dah, died. When Y'hu-dah was consoled he went up to his sheep shearers, he and his friend Hi-rah the A-dul-la-mi (*Adullamite*), to Tim-nah.

(13) And it was told to Ta-mar, saying,

> "Look, your father-in-law is going up to Tim-nah to shear his sheep."

(14) So she removed the clothes of her widowhood and covered herself with the veil and disguised herself. And she sat at the entrance of Ay-na-yim, which was on the way to Tim-nah, for she saw that She-lah was grown but she had not been given to him as a wife.

(15) And Y'hu-dah saw her and reckoned her to be a prostitute, for she had covered her face.

(16) And he turned aside to her at the roadside and said,

> "Please come, let me come in to you,"

for he did not know that she was his daughter-in-law.
And she said,

> "What will you give to me that you may come in to me?"

(17) And he said,

> "I will send a kid from the goats of the flock."

And she said,

> "Only if you give a pledge until you send it."

(18) And he said,

> "What is the pledge that I must give to you?"

And she said,

> "Your seal, your cord, and your staff that is in your hand."

And he gave them to her and went to her. And she conceived by him.

(19) And she arose and left, and she removed her veil from herself and put on the garments of her widowhood.

(20) And Y'hu-dah sent את the kid from the goats by the hand of his friend the A-dul-la-mi (Adullamite) to take back the pledge from the hand of the woman, but he could not find her.

(21) So he asked את the men of her place, saying,

> "Where is that cult prostitute that was at Ay-na-yim by the roadside?"

And they said,

> "There is no cult prostitute here."

(22) Then he returned to Y'hu-dah and said,

> "I could not find her. Moreover, the men of the place said,
>
> 'There is no cult prostitute here.' "

(23) And Y'hu-dah said,

Level One   בְּרֵאשִׁית ~ לח

> "Let her take them for herself, lest we be laughed at. Behold, I sent this kid, וְאַתָּה (and you) could not find her."

Tamar Has Twins

(24) And about three months later it was told to Y'hu-dah,

> "Ta-mar, your daughter-in-law, has played the whore, and now, behold, she has conceived by prostitution."

And Y'hu-dah said,

> "Bring her out and let her be burned."

(25) She was brought out, but she sent to her father-in-law saying,

> "By the man to whom these belong I have conceived."

And she said,

> "Now discern to whom these belong: the seal and cord and the staff."

(26) Then Y'hu-dah recognized them and said,

> "She is more righteous than I, since I did not give her to my son She-lah."

And he did not know her again.

(27) And it happened that at the time she gave birth that, behold, twins were in her womb.

(28) And it happened that at her labor one child put out a hand. And the midwife

Genesis ~ 38

took it and tied a crimson thread on his hand saying,

> *"This one came out first."*

(29) Then his hand drew back and, behold, his brother came out, and she said,

> *"What!* פָּרַצְתָּ פֶּרֶץ *(You have breached a breach) on yourself!"*

And she called his name פֶּרֶץ (*Perez*).

(30) And afterward his brother who had the crimson thread on his hand came out. And his name was called Za-rakh.

Chapter 39

Joseph Serves Potiphar

(1) Now Yo-sef had been brought down to Mitz-ra-yim (*Egypt*), and Po-ti-far, a eunuch of Far-oh, chief of the guards, Mitz-ri (*an Egyptian*), bought him from the hand of the Yish-m'e-lim (*Ishmaelites*) who had brought him down there.

(2) וַיְהִי יהוה (*And YHVH was*) with אֶת Yo-sef, and he became a successful man. And he was in the house of אֲדֹנָיו (*his lord*) the Mitz-ri (*Egyptian*).

(3) And אֲדֹנָיו (*his lord*) observed that יהוה אִתּוֹ (*YHVH was with him*), and everything that was in his hand to do יהוה (*YHVH*) made successful.

(4) And Yo-sef found favor in his eyes and he served אֹתוֹ (* *him*). Then he appointed him over his house and all that he owned he put into his hand.

(5) And it happened that from the time he appointed אֹתוֹ (* *him*) over his house and over all that he had וַיְבָרֶךְ יהוה (*and YHVH blessed*) אֶת the house of the Mitz-ri (*Egyptian*) on account of Yo-sef. And the blessing of יהוה (*YHVH*) was upon all that he had in the house and in the field.

(6) And he left all that he had in the hand of Yo-sef, and he did not worry about anything with אִתּוֹ (* *him*) except the food that he ate. Now Yo-sef was well built and handsome.

Joseph Wrongly Accused

(7) And it happened that after these things the wife of אֲדֹנָיו (*his lord*) cast אֶת her eyes on Yo-sef, and she said,

> "*Lie with me.*"

(8) But he refused and said to the wife of אֲדֹנָיו (*his lord*),

"Behold אֲדֹנִי (my lord) does not worry concerning אִתִּי (* me). What is in the house, and everything he owns he has put in my hand."

(9)

"He has no greater authority in this house than me, and he has not withheld anything from me except אוֹתָךְ (* you), since אַתְּ (you) are his wife. Now how could I do this great הָרָעָה (evil) and sin לֵאלֹהִים (to Elohim)?"

(10) And it happened that as she spoke to Yo-sef day after day, he did not heed her to lie beside her or to be with her.

(11) But one particular day he came into the house to do his work and none of the men of the house were there in the house.

(12) She seized him by his garment and said,

"Lie with me."

And he left his garment in her hand and fled, and he went outside.

(13) And it happened that when she saw that he left his garment in her hand and fled outside,

(14) she called to the men of her house and said to them,

"Look! He brought an Iv-ri (Hebrew) man to us to mock us! He came to me to lie with me, and I cried out with a loud voice."

(15)

"And when he heard me, that I raised my voice and called out, he left his garment beside me and fled, and he went outside."

(16) Then she put his garment beside her until אֲדֹנָיו (his lord) came to his

Level One   בְּרֵאשִׁית ~ לט

house.

(17) Then she spoke to him according to these words, saying,

> "The Iv-ri (Hebrew) slave that you brought to us came to me to make fun of me."

(18)

> "And it happened that as I raised my voice and called out, he left his garment beside me and fled outside."

(19) And when אֲדֹנָיו (*his lord*) heard אֵת the words of his wife that she spoke to him,

> "This is what your servant did to me,"

he became very angry.

Joseph Put In Prison

(20) And אֲדֹנֵי יוֹסֵף (*the lord of Joseph*) took אֹתוֹ (** him*) and gave him to the house of the prison, the place that the king's prisoners were confined. And he was there in the house of the prison.

(21) וַיְהִי יהוה (*And YHVH was*) with אֵת Yo-sef וַיֵּט (*and He showed*) kindness to him וַיִּתֵּן (*and He gave*) him favor in the eyes of the chief of the house of the prison.

(22) And the chief of the house of the prison put אֵת all the prisoners that were in the prison into the hand of Yo-sef וְאֵת (*and **) everything that was done there, he was the one who did it.

(23) The chief of the house of the prison did not worry about אֵת anything in his hand, since יהוה אִתּוֹ (*YHVH was with him*). And whatever he did יהוה (*YHVH*) made it successful.

Chapter 40

Chief Cupbearer And Chief Baker

(1) And it happened that after these things the cupbearer of the king of Mitz-ra-yim (Egypt) and his baker did offense לַאֲדֹנֵיהֶם (*to their lord*) the king of Mitz-ra-yim (*Egypt*).

(2) And Far-oh was angry with his two eunuchs, with the chief of cupbearers and the chief of bakers.

(3) And he gave אֹתָם (* *them*) in custody in the house of the chief of the guards, into the house of the prison where Yo-sef was confined.

(4) And the chief of the guard appointed אֵת Yo-sef to be with אִתָּם (* *them*), and he attended אֹתָם (* *them*). And they were in custody many days.

(5) And the two of them, the cupbearer and the baker of the king of Mitz-ra-yim (*Egypt*), who were confined in the prison, dreamed a dream, each his own dream, with its own interpretation.

(6) When Yo-sef came to them in the morning and seeing אֹתָם (* *them*), and behold, they were troubled.

(7) And he asked אֶת the eunuchs of Far-oh that were with אִתּוֹ (* *him*) in the custody of the house of אֲדֹנָיו (*his lord*),

> "Why are your faces רָעִים (*evil ones*) today?"

(8) And they said to him,

> "We each dreamed a dream, but there is no one to interpret אֹתוֹ (* *it*)."

Level One
בְּרֵאשִׁית ~ מ

And Yo-sef said to them,

> "Do not interpretations belong לֵאלֹהִים (to Elohim)? Tell them to me."

Chief Cupbearer's Dream

(9) Then the chief of the cupbearers told אֵת his dream to Yo-sef, and he said to him,

> "In my dream, now behold, there was a vine before me."

(10)

> "And on the vine were three branches. And as it budded, its blossoms came up, and its clusters of grapes grew ripe."

(11)

> "And the cup of Far-oh was in my hand, and I took אֵת the grapes and squeezed אֹתָם (* them) into the cup of Far-oh. Then I placed אֵת the cup into the palm of Far-oh."

(12) Then Yo-sef said to him,

> "This is its interpretation: The three branches, they are three days."

(13)

> "In three days Far-oh will lift up אֵת your head and will restore you to your post. And you shall put the cup of Far-oh into his hand as was formerly the custom, when you were his cupbearer."

(14)

> "But remember me when it goes well with אִתָּךְ (* you), and please may you show kindness with respect to me, and mention me to

> Far-oh, and bring me from of this house."

(15)
> "For I was surely kidnapped from the land of the Iv-rim (Hebrews), and here also I have done nothing that they put אֹתִי (* me) in the dungeon."

Chief Baker's Dream

(16) And when the chief of the bakers saw that the interpretation was טוֹב (*good*), he said to Yo-sef,

> "I also dreamed. In my dream, now behold, there were three baskets of bread upon my head."

(17)
> "And in the upper basket, from all the food of Far-oh, the work of a baker, and the flyer ate אֹתָם (* them) out of the basket from on my head."

(18) Then Yo-sef answered and said,

> "This is its interpretation: The three baskets, they are three days."

(19)
> "In three days Far-oh will lift אֶת your head from you and hang אוֹתְךָ (* you) on a tree, and the flyer will eat אֶת your flesh from you."

(20) And it happened that on the third day, which was the birthday of אֶת Far-oh, he made a feast for all his servants. And he lifted up אֶת the head of the

Level One — בְּרֵאשִׁית ~ מ

chief of the cupbearers וְאֵת (and *) the head of the chief of the bakers in the midst of his servants.

(21) And he restored אֶת the chief of the cupbearers to his cupbearing position. And he placed the cup in the palm of Far-oh.

(22) וְאֵת (and *) the chief of the bakers he hanged as Yo-sef had interpreted to them.

(23) But the chief cupbearer did not remember אֶת Yo-sef, but forgot him.

Chapter 41

Pharaoh's Dreams

(1) And it happened that after two full years, Far-oh dreamed, and behold, he was standing by the river.

(2) And behold, seven cows, lovely of appearance and plump of flesh, were coming up from the river, and they grazed among the reeds.

(3) And behold, seven other cows came up after them from the river רָעוֹת (*evil ones*) of appearance and thin of flesh, and they stood beside those cows on the bank of the river.

(4) And the cows רָעוֹת (*evil ones*) of appearance and thin of flesh, ate אֶת the seven cows lovely of appearance and fat. And Far-oh awoke.

(5) And he fell asleep and dreamed a second time, and behold, seven ears of grain, plump וְטֹבוֹת (*and good ones*), were coming out of one stalk.

(6) And behold, seven thin ears of grain, scorched by the east wind, sprouted up after them.

(7) And the thin ears of grain swallowed up אֵת the seven plump and full ears of grain. And Far-oh awoke, and behold, it was a dream.

(8) And it happened that in the morning רוּחוֹ (*his spirit*) was troubled, and he sent and called אֶת all of the sacred scribes of Mitz-ra-yim (*Egypt*) וְאֶת (*and **) all its wise men, and Far-oh told אֶת his dream to them. And there was no one who could interpret אוֹתָם (** them*) for Far-oh.

Joseph Meets Pharaoh

(9) Then the chief of the cupbearers spoke with אֶת Far-oh, saying,

Level One   בְּרֵאשִׁית ~ מא

> "I remember אֵת my sins today."

(10)

> "Far-oh was angry with his servants, and he gave אֹתִי (* me) in the custody of the house of the chief of the guard וְאֵת (* me) (and *) the chief the bakers."

(11)

> "And we dreamed a dream one night, I and he, each man according to the interpretation of his dream, we dreamed."

(12)

> "And there with אִתָּנוּ (* us) was a young man, an Iv-ri (Hebrew) servant to the chief of the guard, and we related to him and he interpreted for us אֵת our dreams, each according to his dream he interpreted."

(13)

> "And it happened just as he interpreted to us, so it was -- אֹתִי (* me), he restored to my post וְאֹתוֹ (and * him), he hanged."

(14) And Far-oh sent and called אֵת Yo-sef, and they brought him quickly from the dungeon. And he shaved and changed his clothing, and came to Far-oh.

(15) Then Far-oh said to Yo-sef,

> "I dreamed a dream, but there is none to interpret אֹתוֹ (* it). And I have heard concerning you that when you hear a dream you can interpret אֹתוֹ (* it)."

(16) Then Yo-sef answered אֵת Far-oh saying,

> "Apart from me אֱלֹהִים יַעֲנֶה (Elohim will answer) אֶת-שְׁלוֹם

229

Genesis ~ 41

פַּרְעֹה *(* the peace of Pharaoh)."*

Pharaoh Tells Joseph His Dreams

(17) And Far-oh said to Yo-sef,

"In my dream, behold, I was standing on the bank of the river."

(18)

"And behold, from the river, seven cows, plump of flesh and lovely of shape, were coming up, and they grazed among the reeds."

(19)

"And behold, seven other cows came up after them, very poor ones וְרָעוֹת *(and evil ones of)* shape, and exceedingly emaciated of flesh -- never have I seen any as them in all the land of Mitz-ra-yim (Egypt) לָרֹעַ *(for the evil)*."

(20)

"And the cows, the thin וְהָרָעוֹת *(and the evil ones)* ate אֵת the seven cows, the first ones, the plump ones."

(21)

"And they went into their bellies and it was not known that they went into their bellies, and their appearance was as רַע *(evil)* as at the start. And I awoke."

(22)

"And I saw in my dream and behold, seven ears of grain were coming out of one stalk, full וְטֹבוֹת *(and good ones)*."

(23)

230

| Level One | בְּרֵאשִׁית ~ מא |

"And behold, seven withered ears of grain, thin and scorched by the east wind, sprouted up after them."

(24)

"And the thin ears of grain swallowed up אֵת the seven ears הַטֹּבוֹת (the good ones) of grain. And I told the sacred scribes, but there was none to explain it to me."

Joseph Interprets Pharaoh's Dreams

(25) Then Yo-sef said to Far-oh,

"The dreams of Far-oh are one. אֵת what הָאֱלֹהִים עֹשֶׂה (the Elohim is doing) הִגִּיד (He has told) to Far-oh."

(26)

"The seven cows הַטֹּבֹת (the good ones), they are seven years, and the seven ears הַטֹּבֹת (the good ones) of grain, they are seven years. It is one dream."

(27)

"And the seven cows, the thin וְהָרָעוֹת (and the evil ones) coming up after them, they are seven years, and the seven empty ears of grain, scorched by the east wind, they are seven years of famine."

(28)

"It is the word that I have spoken to Far-oh, what הָאֱלֹהִים עֹשֶׂה (the Elohim is doing) הֶרְאָה (He has shown) אֵת Far-oh."

(29)

"Behold, seven years of great abundance are coming throughout the whole land of Mitz-ra-yim (Egypt)."

Genesis ~ 41

(30)

"Then seven years of famine will arise after them, and all the abundance in the land of Mitz-ra-yim (Egypt) will be forgotten. And the famine will consume אֶת the land."

(31)

"And abundance in the land will not be known because of the famine that follows, for it will be very grievous."

(32)

"And concerning the repetition of the dream twice to Far-oh, it is because the matter is from הָאֱלֹהִים (the Elohim) and הָאֱלֹהִים לַעֲשֹׂתוֹ (the Elohim will do it) quickly."

(33)

"Now then, let Far-oh select a man who is discerning and wise, and let him set him over the land of Mitz-ra-yim (Egypt)."

(34)

"Let Far-oh do this, and let him appoint supervisors over the land, and let him take one-fifth of אֶת the land of Mitz-ra-yim (Egypt) in the seven years of abundance."

(35)

"Then let them gather אֶת all the food of these coming years הַטֹּבֹת (the good ones), and let them pile up grain under the hand of Far-oh for food in the cities, and let them keep it."

(36)

"Then the food shall be as a deposit for the land for the seven years of the famine that will be in the land of Mitz-ra-yim (Egypt), that the land will not perish on account of the famine."

Level One   בְּרֵאשִׁית ~ מא

(37) And the plan was good in the eyes of Far-oh and in the eyes of all his servants.

Joseph Made Ruler

(38) Then Far-oh said to his servants,

> "Can we find a man like this in whom is רוּחַ אֱלֹהִים (the Spirit of Elohim)?"

(39) Then Far-oh said to Yo-sef,

> "Since אֱלֹהִים (Elohim) has made known to אוֹתְךָ (* you) אֵת all of this, there is no one as discerning and wise as you."

(40)

> אַתָּה (You) shall be over my house, and to your word all my people shall submit. Only with respect to the throne will I be greater than you."

(41) Then Far-oh said to Yo-sef,

> "See, I have set אֹתְךָ (* you) over all the land of Mitz-ra-yim (Egypt)."

(42) Then Far-oh removed אֵת his signet ring from his hand and put אֹתָה (* her) on the hand of Yo-sef. And he clothed אֹתוֹ (* him) with garments of fine linen, and he put a chain of gold around his neck.

(43) And he had אֹתוֹ (* him) ride in his second chariot. And they cried out before him,

> "Kneel!"

Genesis ~ 41

And Far-oh set אֹתוֹ (* him) over all the land of Mitz-ra-yim (*Egypt*).

(44) Then Far-oh said to Yo-sef,

> "I am Far-oh, but without your consent no one will lift אֶת his hand וְאֶת (and *) his foot in all the land of Mitz-ra-yim (*Egypt*)."

(45) And Far-oh called the name of Yo-sef Zaf-nat~Pa-ne-akh and gave him אֶת As-nat, the daughter of Po-ti~fe-ra, priest of On, as a wife. And Yo-sef went out over the land of Mitz-ra-yim (*Egypt*).

Seven Years Of Plenty

(46) Now Yo-sef was thirty years old when he stood before Far-oh, the king of Mitz-ra-yim (*Egypt*). And Yo-sef went out from the presence of Far-oh and traveled through the whole land of Mitz-ra-yim (*Egypt*).

(47) And the land produced plenty in the seven years of abundance.

(48) And he gathered אֶת all the food of the seven years which occurred in the land of Mitz-ra-yim (*Egypt*). And he stored the food in the cities. The food of the field that surrounded each city he stored in its midst.

(49) And Yo-sef piled up grain like the sand of the sea in great abundance until he stopped counting it, for it could not be counted.

Sons Of Joseph

(50) Before the years of famine came, As-nat, daughter of Po-ti~fe-ra priest of On, bore two sons to him.

(51) And Yo-sef called אֵת the name of the firstborn מְנַשֶּׁה (*Manasseh*) for he said,

Level One

בְּרֵאשִׁית ~ מא

"Because נַשַּׁנִי אֱלֹהִים (Elohim has caused me to forget) אֵת all my hardship וְאֵת (and *) all my father's house."

(52) וְאֵת (and *) the name of the second he called אֶפְרָיִם (Ephraim) for he said,

"Because הִפְרַנִי אֱלֹהִים (Elohim has made me fruitful) in the land of my misfortune."

Seven Years Of Famine

(53) And the seven years of abundance which were in the land of Mitz-ra-yim (*Egypt*) came to an end.

(54) And the seven years of famine began to come as Yo-sef had said. And there was famine in all of the countries, but in the land of Mitz-ra-yim (*Egypt*) there was food.

(55) And when all the land of Mitz-ra-yim (*Egypt*) was hungry the people cried out to Far-oh for food. And Far-oh said to all the land of Mitz-ra-yim (*Egypt*),

"Go to Yo-sef; what he says to you, you must do."

(56) And the famine was over the whole land, and Yo-sef opened אֵת all the storehouses and sold food to Mitz-ra-yim (*Egypt*). And the famine was severe in the land of Mitz-ra-yim (*Egypt*).

(57) And every land came to Mitz-ra-yim (*Egypt*) to Yo-sef to buy grain, for the famine was severe in every land.

Chapter 42

Joseph's Brothers Come To Egypt

(1) And Ya-a-kov (Jacob) realized that there was grain in Mitz-ra-yim (Egypt), Ya-a-kov (Jacob) said to his sons,

> "Why do you look at one another?"

(2) And he said,

> "Look, I have heard that there is grain in Mitz-ra-yim (Egypt). Go down there and buy grain for us there that we may live and not die."

(3) And the ten brothers of Yo-sef went down to buy grain from Mitz-ra-yim (*Egypt*).

(4) וְאֶת (*and **) Ben-ya-min, the brother of Yo-sef, Ya-a-kov (*Jacob*) did not send with אֶת his brothers because he said,

> "Lest mishap would come to him."

(5) And the sons of Yis-ra-el went to buy grain amid those other people who went as well, for there was famine in the land of K'na-an.

(6) And Yo-sef was the governor over the land. He was the one who sold food to all the people of the land. And the brothers of Yo-sef came and bowed down to him with their faces to the ground.

(7) And Yo-sef saw אֶת his brothers and recognized them, but he pretended to be a stranger to them. And he spoke with אֹתָם (** them*) harshly and said to them,

Level One   בְּרֵאשִׁית ~ מב

> "From where have you come?"

And they said,

> "From the land of K'na-an to buy food."

(8) And Yo-sef recognized אֶת his brothers, but they did not recognize him.

(9) And Yo-sef remembered אֶת the dreams which he had dreamed concerning them, and he said to them,

> אַתֶּם (You) are spies! You have come to see אֶת the nakedness of the land!"

(10) And they said to him,

> "No אֲדֹנִי (my lord) but your servants have come to buy food."

(11)

> "We all are sons of one man. We are honest men. We, your servants, are not spies."

(12) Then he said to them,

> "No, but you have come to see the nakedness of the land."

(13) Then they said,

> "We, your servants, are twelve brothers, the sons of one man in the land of K'na-an, and behold, the youngest is with אֶת our father today, and one is no more."

(14) But Yo-sef said to them,

> "It is what I said to you -- אַתֶּם (you) are spies."

(15)
> "By this you shall be tested. By the life of Far-oh you will not go out from here unless your youngest brother comes here."

(16)
> "Send one of you, and let him bring אֶת your brother, but you will be kept in prison so that your words might be tested to see if there is truth with אִתְּכֶם (* you). And if not, by the life of Far-oh surely אַתֶּם (you) are spies."

(17) Then he gathered אֹתָם (* them) into the prison for three days.

(18) On the third day Yo-sef said to them,

> "Do this and you will live; I fear אֶת-הָאֱלֹהִים (the Elohim)."

(19)
> "If אַתֶּם (you) are honest, let one of your brothers be kept in prison where you are now being kept, but the rest of you go, carry grain for the famine for your households."

(20)
> וְאֶת (and *) your brother, the youngest one, you must bring to me, and then your words will be confirmed and you will not die."

And they did so.

(21) Then each said to his brother,

> "Surely we are guilty on account of our brother when we saw the anguish of his soul when he pleaded for mercy to us and we would not listen. Therefore, this trouble has come to us."

(22) Then R'u-ven answered אֹתָם (* them), saying,

Level One

בְּרֵאשִׁית ~ מב

> *"Did I not say to you, do not sin against the boy? But you did not listen, and now, behold, his blood has been sought."*

(23) Now they did not know that Yo-sef understood, for the interpreter was between them.

(24) And he turned away from them and wept. Then he returned to them and spoke to them, and he took מֵאִתָּם (*from them*) אֶת Shim-on and bound אֹתוֹ (* *him*) in front of them.

The Brothers Return Home

(25) Then Yo-sef gave orders to fill אֶת their vessels with grain and to return their money to each sack, and to give them provisions for the journey. Thus he did for them.

(26) Then they loaded אֶת their grain upon their donkeys and went away from there.

(27) And one of them later opened אֶת his sack to give fodder to his donkey at the lodging place and saw אֶת his money -- behold, it was in the mouth of his sack.

(28) And he said to his brothers,

> *"My money was returned and moreover, behold, it is in my sack!"*

Then their hearts failed them and each of them trembled and said,

> *"What is this* עָשָׂה אֱלֹהִים *(Elohim has done) to us?"*

(29) And when they came to Ya-a-kov (*Jacob*) their father in the land of K'na-an they told him אֶת everything that had happened to אֹתָם (* *them*), saying,

239

(30)

"The man אֲדֹנֵי הָאָרֶץ (the lord of the land), spoke harshly with אִתָּנוּ (* us) and treated אֹתָנוּ (* us) as if we were spying out אֵת the land."

(31)

"But we said to him,

'We are honest; we are not spies.' "

(32)

'We are twelve brothers, the sons of our father. One is no more and the youngest is with אֶת our father in the land of K'na-an.' "

(33)

"Then the man אֲדֹנֵי הָאָרֶץ (the lord of the land), said to us,

'By this I will know that אַתֶּם (you) are honest. Leave one brother with אִתִּי (* me) וְאֵת (and *) the famine in your households, take food and go.' "

(34)

'And bring אֶת your brother, the youngest one, to me. Then I will know that אַתֶּם (you) are not spies, that אַתֶּם (you) are honest. And I will give אֶת your brother back to you, וְאֶת (and *) the land, you can be merchants.' "

(35) And it happened that when they emptied their sacks, behold, each one's pouch of money was in his sack. And when they and their father saw אֵת the pouches of their money, they were greatly distressed.

(36) And Ya-a-kov (Jacob) their father said to them,

Level One   בְּרֵאשִׁית ~ מב

"You have bereaved אֹתִי (* me). Yo-sef is no more and Shim-on is no more וְאֶת (and *) Ben-ya-min you would take! All of this is against me!"

(37) And R'u-ven said to his father,

"You may kill אֶת two of my sons if I do not bring him back to you. Give אֹתוֹ (* him) in my hand and I myself will return him to you."

(38) But he said,

"My son shall not go down with you, for his brother is dead and he alone remains. If harm meets him on the journey that you would take, you would bring down אֶת my gray hairs in sorrow to Sh'ol."

Chapter 43

Back To Egypt

(1) Now the famine in the land was severe.

(2) And it happened that as they finished eating אֵת the grain which they had brought from Mitz-ra-yim (*Egypt*) their father said to them,

> "Return and buy a little food for us."

(3) Then Y'hu-dah said to him,

> "The man solemnly admonished us, saying,
>> 'You shall not see my face unless your brother is with אִתְּכֶם (** you*).' "

(4)

> "If you will send אֵת our brother with אִתָּנוּ (** us*), we will go down and buy food for you."

(5)

> "And if you will not send him, we will not go down, for the man said to us,
>> 'You shall not see my face unless your brother is with אִתְּכֶם (** you*).' "

(6) Then Yis-ra-el said,

> "Why did you bring trouble to me by telling the man you still had a brother?"

Level One   בְּרֵאשִׁית ~ מג

(7) And they said,

> "The man asked explicitly about us and about our family, saying,
>
> 'Is your father still alive? Do you have a brother?'
>
> "And we answered him according to these words. How could we know that he would say,
>
> 'Bring down אֶת your brother.'?"

(8) Then Y'hu-dah said to his father Yis-ra-el,

> "Send the young man with אִתִּי (* me), and let us arise and go, so that we will live and not die -- we, also אַתָּה (you), also our children."

(9)

> "I myself will be surety for him, you may seek him from my hand. If I do not bring him back to you and present him before you, then I will stand guilty before you forever."

(10)

> "Surely if we had not hesitated by this time, we would have returned twice."

(11) Then their father Yis-ra-el said to them,

> "If it must be so, then do this. Take some of the best products of the land in your bags and take them down to the man as a gift -- a little balm and honey, aromatic gum and myrrh, and pistachios and almonds."

Genesis ~ 43

(12)

"And take double the money in your hands. וְאֵת (and *) themoney that was returned in the mouth of your sacks, you shall restore. Perhaps it was a mistake."

(13)

וְאֶת (and *) your brother -- take, arise, and return to the man."

(14)

וְאֵל שַׁדַּי יִתֵּן (And El Almighty give) you compassion before the man וְשִׁלַּח (and he may send) אֶת your other brother to you וְאֶת (and *) Ben-ya-min. As for me, if I am bereaved, I am bereaved."

(15) So the men took this אֵת gift, and they took double money in their hands וְאֶת (and *) Ben-ya-min, and they rose up and went down to Mitz-ra-yim (*Egypt*) and stood before Yo-sef.

Brothers Brought To Joseph's House

(16) When Yo-sef saw אֶת Ben-ya-min with אִתָּם (* *them*), he said to the one who was over his household,

"Bring אֶת the men into the house and slaughter and prepare an animal, for the men shall eat with אִתִּי (* *me*) at noon."

(17) And the man did as Yo-sef had said, and the man brought אֶת the men into the house of Yo-sef.

(18) And the men were afraid when they were brought into the house of Yo-sef. And they said

"We were brought here on account of the money that was returned

Level One   בְּרֵאשִׁית ~ מג

to our sacks the first time, that he might attack us and fall upon us to take אֹתָנוּ (* us) for servants וְאֵת (and *) our donkeys."

(19) So they approached the man who was over the house of Yo-sef and spoke to him at the doorway of the house.

(20) And they said,

"Please אֲדֹנִי (my lord), we surely came down once before to buy food."

(21)

"And when we came to the place of lodging and we opened אֶת our sacks, then behold, each one's money was in the mouth of his sack -- our money in its full weight -- so we have returned with אֹתוֹ (* it) in our hands."

(22)

"And, other money we have brought down in our hand to buy food. We do not know who put our money in our sacks."

(23) And he said,

שָׁלוֹם לָכֶם (Peace to you); do not be afraid. אֱלֹהֵיכֶם (Your Elohim) וֵאלֹהֵי אֲבִיכֶם (and the Elohim of your father) נָתַן (He gave) you a treasure in your sacks; your money came to me."

And he brought אֶת Shim-on out to them.

(24) Then the man brought אֶת the men to the house of Yo-sef and he gave them water and washed their feet, and gave fodder to their donkeys.

(25) Then they prepared אֶת the gift until Yo-sef came at noon, for they had heard that they were to eat food there.

Joseph Eats With His Brothers

(26) And when Yo-sef came into the house, they brought אֵת the gift that was in their hand into the house to him, and they bowed down before him to the ground.

(27) And he greeted them and asked them לְשָׁלוֹם (for peace),

> הֲשָׁלוֹם (The peace of) your father, the old man of whom you spoke? Is he still alive?"

(28) And they said,

> "Your servant our father is שָׁלוֹם (peace) he is still alive."

And they knelt and bowed down.

(29) Then he lifted up his eyes and saw אֵת Ben-ya-min his brother, the son of his mother, and said,

> "Is this your youngest brother of whom you told me?"

And he continued,

> אֱלֹהִים יָחְנְךָ (Elohim be gracious to you), my son."

(30) Then Yo-sef hurried away, being overcome with emotion toward his brother, and sought for a place to cry. Then he went into a room and wept there.

(31) Then he washed his face and went out, now controlling himself, and said,

> "Serve the food."

(32) And they set a place for him by himself, and for them by themselves, and for the Mitz-rim (*Egyptians*) who were eating with אִתּוֹ (*him*) by themselves -- for Mitz-rim (Egyptians) could not dine with אֵת the Iv-rim (*Hebrews*), because that was a detestable thing to Mitz-ra-yim (*Egypt*).

Level One   בְּרֵאשִׁית ~ מג

(33) And they were seated before him from the firstborn according to his birthright to the youngest according to his youth. And the men looked at one another amazed.

(34) And he lifted up portions מֵאֵת (*from* *) in front of him to them, and the portion of Ben-ya-min was five times greater than the portion of any of them. And they drank and became drunk with him.

Chapter 44

Joseph's Cup

(1) Then he commanded the one אֶת who was over his household, saying,

> "Fill אֶת the sacks of the men with food as much as they are able to carry, and put each one's money in the mouth of his sack."

(2)

> וְאֶת (and *) my cup, the cup of silver, you shall put into the mouth of the sack of the youngest וְאֶת (and *) the money for his grain."

And he did according to the word of Yo-sef that he had commanded.

(3) When the morning light came the men were sent away, they and their donkeys.

(4) They went out of אֶת the city, and had not gone far when Yo-sef said to the one who was over his house,

> "Arise! Pursue after the men and overtake them. Then you shall say to them,
>
>> 'Why have you repaid רָעָה תַּחַת טוֹבָה (evil instead of good)?'"

(5)

>> 'Is this not that from which אֲדֹנִי (my lord) drinks? Now he himself certainly practices divination with it. הֲרֵעֹתֶם (You did evil) in what you have done.'"

(6) When he overtook them, he spoke אֶת these words to them.

Level One   בְּרֵאשִׁית ~ מד

(7) And they said to him,

> "Why has אֲדֹנִי (my lord) spoken according to these words? Far be it from your servants to do such a thing!"

(8)

> "Behold, the money that we found in the mouth of our sacks we returned to you from the land of K'na-an. Now why would we steal from the house of אֲדֹנֶיךָ (your lord) silver or gold?"

(9)

> "Whoever is found with אִתּוֹ (* it) from among your servants shall die. And moreover, we will become servants לַאדֹנִי (to my lord)."

(10) Then he said,

> "Now also according to your words, thus will it be. He who is found with אִתּוֹ (* it) shall be my slave, and you shall be innocent."

(11) Then each man quickly brought down אֶת his sack to the ground, and each one opened his sack.

(12) And he searched, beginning with the oldest and finishing with the youngest. And the cup was found in the sack of Ben-ya-min.

(13) Then they tore their clothes, and each one loaded his donkey and they returned to the city.

Judah Pleads With Joseph

(14) And Y'hu-dah and his brothers came to the house of Yo-sef -- now he was still there -- they fell before him to the ground.

(15) Then Yo-sef said to them,

"What is this deed that you have done? Did you not know that a man who is like me surely practices divination?"

(16) And Y'hu-dah said,

"What can we say לַאדֹנִי (to my lord)? What can we speak? Now how can we show ourselves innocent? הָאֱלֹהִים מָצָא (the Elohim has found) אֶת the guilt of your servants! Behold, we are servants לַאדֹנִי (to my lord) both we and also he in whose hand the cup was found."

(17) But he said,

"Far be it from me to do this! The man in whose hand the cup was found, he will become my slave. But as for you, go up לְשָׁלוֹם (to peace) to your father."

(18) But Y'hu-dah drew near to him and said,

"Please אֲדֹנִי (my lord), let your servant speak a word in the ears of אֲדֹנִי (my lord) and let not your anger burn against your servant, for you are like Far-oh himself."

(19)

אֲדֹנִי (My lord) had asked אֶת his servants, saying,

'Do you have a father or a brother?' "

(20)

"And we said to אֲדֹנִי (my lord),

'We have an aged father, and a younger brother, the child of his old age, and his brother died, and he alone remains from

Level One   בְּרֵאשִׁית ~ מד

his mother, and his father loves him.' "

(21)

"Then you said to your servants,

'Bring him down to me that I may set my eyes upon him.'

(22)

"Then we said to אֲדֹנִי (my lord),

'The boy cannot leave אֶת his father; if he should leave אֶת his father, then he would die.' "

(23)

"Then you said to your servants,

'Unless your youngest brother comes down with אִתְּכֶם (* you), you shall not again see my face.' "

(24)

"And it happened that we went up to your servant, my father, and told him אֵת the words of אֲדֹנִי (my lord)."

(25)

"And when our father said,

'Buy a little food for us,' "

(26)

"Then we said,

'We cannot go down. If our youngest brother is with אִתָּנוּ (* us), then we shall go down. For we will not be able to see the face of the man unless our youngest brother is with אִתָּנוּ (* us).' "

Genesis ~ 44

(27)
"Then your servant, my father, said to us,

'You yourselves know that my wife bore two sons to me.'

(28)
'One went out מֵאִתִּי (from * me), and I said,

"Surely he must have been torn to pieces,"

'and I have never seen him since.' "

(29)
'And if you also take אֶת this one also from me, and he encounters harm, you will bring down אֶת my gray hairs בְּרָעָה (in evil) to Sh'ol.' "

(30)
"So now, when I come to your servant, my father, and the young man is not with אִתָּנוּ (* us), now his soul is bound up with his soul."

(31)
"It shall happen that when he sees that the boy is gone, he will die. And your servants will bring down אֶת the gray hairs of your servant, our father, to Sh'ol with sorrow."

(32)
"For your servant is pledged as surety for אֶת the young man by my father, saying,

'If I do not bring him to you, then I shall have sinned to my father forever.' "

Level One   בְּרֵאשִׁית ~ מד

(33) "So then, please let your servant remain in place of the boy as a slave לַאדֹנִי (to my lord), and let the young man go up with his brothers."

(34) "For how can I go up to my father if the young man is not with אִתִּי (*me)? Lest I look בָרָע (on evil) which will find אֶת my father."

Chapter 45

Joseph Reunites With His Brothers

(1) Then Yo-sef was not able to control himself before all who were standing by him. And he cried out,

"Make every man go out from me!"

So no man stood with אֹתוֹ (* *him*) when Yo-sef made himself known to his brothers.

(2) And he אֶת wept loudly, so that Mitz-ra-yim (*Egypt*) heard it and the household of Far-oh heard it.

(3) Then Yo-sef said to his brothers,

"I am Yo-sef! Is my father still alive?"

And his brothers were unable to answer אֹתוֹ (* *him*), for they were flustered at his presence.

(4) So Yo-sef said to his brothers,

"Come near to me, please."

And they drew near. And he said,

"I am Yo-sef, your brother, you sold אֹתִי *(* me*) to Mitz-ra-yim (Egypt)."*

(5)

"So now, do not be distressed and do not be angry with yourselves that you sold אֹתִי *(* me*) here, for* שְׁלָחַנִי אֱלֹהִים *(Elohim sent me) as deliverance before you."*

Level One   בְּרֵאשִׁית ~ מה

(6)

"For these two years the famine has been in the midst of the land, but there will be five more years where there is no plowing or harvest."

(7)

וַיִּשְׁלָחֵנִי אֱלֹהִים (And Elohim sent me) before you all לָשׂוּם (to place) for you a remnant in the land וּלְהַחֲיוֹת (and to preserve alive) for you for a great deliverance."

(8)

"And now אַתֶּם (you) yourselves did not send אֹתִי (* me) here, but הָאֱלֹהִים (the Elohim) וַיְשִׂימֵנִי (and He put me) for a father to Far-oh וּלְאָדוֹן (and for a lord) to all his household, and a ruler over all the land of Mitz-ra-yim (Egypt)."

(9)

"Hurry, and go up to my father and say to him,

'Thus says your son Yo-sef שָׂמַנִי אֱלֹהִים (Elohim has placed me) לְאָדוֹן לְכָל-מִצְרָיִם (for a lord of all Mitz-ra-yim/Egypt). Come down to me and do not delay.'

(10)

'You shall settle in the land of Go-shen so that you will be near me אַתָּה (you) and your children and your grand children, and your flocks and your herds and all that you have.'

(11)

'And I will sustain אֹתְךָ (* you) there, because there are still five years of famine, lest אַתָּה (you) and your household and all that you have become destitute.'

Genesis ~ 45

(12)
> "Now behold, your eyes see, and the eyes of my brother Ben-ya-min see, that it is I who am speaking to you."

(13)
> "And you must tell my father of אֵת all my honor in Mitz-ra-yim (Egypt) וְאֵת (and *) all that you have seen. Now hurry and bring אֶת my father here."

(14) Then he fell upon the neck of his brother Ben-ya-min and wept, and Ben-ya-min wept upon his neck.

(15) And he kissed all his brothers and wept upon them. And afterward his brothers spoke with אִתוֹ (* him).

(16) Then the report was heard in the house of Far-oh, saying,

> "The brothers of Yo-sef have come."

And it pleased Far-oh and his servants.

(17) Then Far-oh said to Yo-sef,

> "Say to your brothers:
>
>> 'Do this: load אֶת your beasts and go back to the land of K'na-an.'

(18)
>> 'And take אֶת your father וְאֶת (and *) your households and come to me, and I will give you אֶת-טוֹב (* the good of)the land of Mitz-ra-yim (Egypt), and you shall eat אֵת the fat of the land.'

Level One   בְּרֵאשִׁית ~ מה

(19)

וְאַתָּה (And you) Yo-sef, are commanded to say this:

'Do this! Take wagons from the land of Mitz-ra-yim (Egypt) for your little ones and your wives, and bring אֶת your father and come.'

(20)

'Do not worry about your possessions for טוּב (the good) of all the land of Mitz-ra-yim (Egypt) is yours.' "

Brothers Sent To Jacob

(21) And the sons of Yis-ra-el did so. And Yo-sef gave them wagons at the word of Far-oh, and gave them provisions for the journey.

(22) To each and to all of them he gave sets of clothing, but to Ben-ya-min he gave three hundred pieces of silver and five sets of clothing.

(23) And to his father he sent as follows: ten donkeys carrying מִטּוּב (*from the good of*) Mitz-ra-yim (*Egypt*), and ten donkeys carrying grain and food and provisions for his father for the journey.

(24) Then he sent אֶת his brothers away, and when they departed he said to them,

"Do not be upset on the way."

(25) So they went up from Mitz-ra-yim (*Egypt*) and came to the land of K'na-an to Ya-a-kov (*Jacob*) their father.

(26) And they spoke to him, saying,

"Yo-sef is still alive, and he is ruler over all the land of Mitz-ra-yim (*Egypt*)!"

Genesis ~ 45

And his heart went numb, because he did not believe them.

(27) Then they said to him אֶת all the words of Yo-sef that he had spoken to them. And when he saw אֵת the wagons that Yo-sef had sent to carry אֹתוֹ (*him*), then רוּחַ יַעֲקֹב (*the spirit of Jacob*) their father revived.

(28) And Yis-ra-el said,

> "It is enough. Yo-sef my son is still alive. I will go and see him before I die."

Chapter 46

Jacob Goes To Egypt

(1) So Yis-ra-el journeyed with all that he had, and he came to Ber~Sha-va and offered sacrifices לֵאלֹהֵי אָבִיו יִצְחָק (to the Elohim of his father Isaac).

(2) וַיֹּאמֶר אֱלֹהִים לְיִשְׂרָאֵל (And Elohim spoke to Yis-ra-el) in visions of the night וַיֹּאמֶר (and He said)

יַעֲקֹב יַעֲקֹב

Jacob, Jacob

And he said,

"Here I am."

(3) וַיֹּאמֶר (And He said)

אָנֹכִי הָאֵל
אֱלֹהֵי אָבִיךָ
אַל־תִּירָא
מֵרְדָה מִצְרַיְמָה
כִּי־לְגוֹי גָּדוֹל אֲשִׂימְךָ שָׁם

I am the El
the Elohim of your father.
You must not fear
from going down towards Egypt,
because a great nation I will make you there.

(4)

אָנֹכִי אֵרֵד עִמְּךָ

מִצְרַיְמָה

וְאָנֹכִי אַעַלְךָ גַם-עָלֹה

וְיוֹסֵף יָשִׁית

יָדוֹ עַל-עֵינֶיךָ

I will go down with you

to Egypt,

and I will surely also bring you up. And Joseph will place

his hand over your eyes.

(5) So Ya-a-kov (*Jacob*) arose from Ber~Sha-va. And the sons of Yis-ra-el carried אֶת Ya-a-kov (*Jacob*), their father וְאֶת (*and **) their little ones וְאֶת (*and **) their wives in the wagons Far-oh had sent to transport אֹתוֹ (** him*).

(6) And they took אֶת their livestock וְאֶת (*and **) their possessions that they had acquired in the land of K'na-an. And they came to Mitz-ra-yim (*Egypt*), Ya-a-kov (*Jacob*) and all his seed with אִתּוֹ (** him*),

(7) his sons and his sons' sons with אִתּוֹ (** him*), his daughters and his daughters' daughters with אִתּוֹ (** him*), into Mitz-ra-yim (*Egypt*).

Sons Of Leah

(8) Now these are the names of the sons of Yis-ra-el, who came into Mitz-ra-yim (*Egypt*), Ya-a-kov (*Jacob*) and his sons. R'u-ven, the firstborn of Ya-a-kov (*Jacob*)

(9) and the sons of R'u-ven: Kha-nokh and Fal-lu and Khez-ron and Khar-mi.

Level One

בְּרֵאשִׁית ~ מו

(10) The sons of Shim-on: Y'mu-el, Ya-min and O-had and Ya-khin and Zo-khar and Sha-ul, the son of the C'na-a-nit (Canaanite woman).

(11) The sons of Le-vi: Ger-shon, K'hat and M'ra-ri.

(12) The sons of Y'hu-dah: Er and O-nan and She-lah and Fe-retz and Za-rakh (and Er and O-nan died in the land of K'na-an). And the sons of Fe-retz were Khez-ron and Kha-mul.

(13) The sons of Yis-sas-khar: To-lah and Fu-vah and Yob and Shim-ron.

(14) The sons of Z'vu-lun: Se-red and E-lon, and Yakh-l'el.

(15) These are the sons of Le-ah that she bore to Ya-a-kov (*Jacob*) in Pad-de-nah~A-ram וְאֵת (*and* *) Di-nah his daughter. His sons and daughters were thirty-three persons in all.

Sons Of Zilpah

(16) The sons of Gad: Zif-yon and Khag-gi, Shu-ni and Etz-bon, E-ri and A-ro-di and Ar-e-li.

(17) The sons of A-sher: Yim-nah and Yish-vah and Yish-vi and V'ri-ah and Se-rakh, their sister. And the sons of V'ri-ah: Khe-ver and Mal-ki-el.

(18) There are the sons of Zil-pah, whom La-van gave to Le-ah his daughter, and she bore אֵת these to Ya-a-kov (Jacob) -- sixteen persons.

Sons Of Rachel

(19) The sons of Ra-khel, the wife of Ya-a-kov (*Jacob*): Yo-sef and Ben-ya-min.

(20) And born to Yo-sef in the land of Mitz-ra-yim (*Egypt*), that As-nat, daughter of Po-ti~fe-ra, priest of On bore to him אֵת M'na-sheh וְאֵת (*and* *) Ef-ra-yim.

(21) The sons of Ben-ya-min: Be-la and Ve-kher and Ash-bel, Ge-ra and

Na-a-man and E-khi and Rosh, Mu-fim and Khu-fim and Ar-d'.

(22) These are the sons of Ra-khel who were born to Ya-a-kov (*Jacob*) -- fourteen persons in all.

Sons Of Bilhah

(23) The sons of Dan: Khu-shim.

(24) The sons of Naf-ta-li: Yakh-tz'el and Gu-ni and Ye-tzer and Shil-lem.

(25) These are the sons of Bil-hah whom La-van gave to Ra-khel his daughter, and she bore אֶת these to Ya-a-kov (*Jacob*) -- seven persons in all.

Total In Egypt

(26) All the persons belonging to Ya-a-kov (*Jacob*) who came to Mitz-ra-yim (*Egypt*) who were his descendants, not including the wives of the sons of Ya-a-kov (*Jacob*) were sixty-six persons in all.

(27) And the sons of Yo-sef who were born to him in Mitz-ra-yim (*Egypt*) were two persons. All the persons of the house of Ya-a-kov (*Jacob*) who came to Mitz-ra-yim (*Egypt*) were seventy.

Jacob And Joseph Reunited

(28) וְאֶת (*and* *) Y'hu-dah sent ahead of him to Yo-sef to appear before him in Go-shen. And they came to the land of Go-shen.

(29) Then Yo-sef harnessed his chariot and went up to meet Yis-ra-el his father in Go-shen. He presented himself to him and fell upon his neck and wept upon his neck a long time.

Level One   בְּרֵאשִׁית ~ מו

(30) Then Yis-ra-el said to Yo-sef,

> "Now let me die since I have seen אֶת your face, for you are still alive."

(31) Then Yo-sef said to his brothers and to his father's household,

> "I will go up and report to Far-oh, and I will say to him,
>
>> 'My brothers and my father's household who were in the land of K'na-an have come to me.' "

(32)

>> 'And the men are רֹעֵי (shepherds), for they are men of livestock, and they have brought their flocks and their cattle and all that they have.' "

(33)

> "And it shall be that when Far-oh calls you he will say,
>
>> 'What is your occupation?' "

(34)

> "Then you must say,
>
>> 'You servants are men of livestock from our childhood until now, both we and also our ancestors.'
>
> "So that you may dwell in the land of Go-shen, for every רֹעֵה (shepherd) is a detestable thing to Mitz-ra-yim (Egypt)."

Chapter 47

Pharaoh Meets Israel

(1) So Yo-sef went and reported to Far-oh. And he said,

> "My father and my brothers, with their flocks and their herds, and all that they possess, have come from the land of K'na-an. Now they are here in the land of Go-shen."

(2) And from among his brothers he took five men and presented them before Far-oh.

(3) And Far-oh said to his brothers,

> "What is your occupation?"

And they said to Far-oh,

> "Your servants are רֹעֵה (shepherds of) sheep, both we and also our ancestors."

(4) And they said to Far-oh,

> "We have come to sojourn in the land, for there is no מִרְעֶה (pasture) for your servant's flocks, for the famine is severe in the land of K'na-an. So now, please let your servants dwell in the land of Go-shen."

(5) Then Far-oh said to Yo-sef,

> "Your father and your brothers have come to you."

Level One   בְּרֵאשִׁית ~ מז

(6)
> "The land of Mitz-ra-yim (Egypt) is before you. Settle אֶת your father וְאֶת (and *) your brothers in the best of the land. Let them live in the land of Go-shen, and if you know of any men of ability among them, then appoint them overseers of my own livestock."

(7) Then Yo-sef brought אֶת Ya-a-kov (*Jacob*) his father and presented him before Far-oh. And Ya-a-kov (Jacob) blessed אֶת Far-oh.

(8) Then Far-oh said to Ya-a-kov (*Jacob*),

> "How old are you?"

(9) And Ya-a-kov (*Jacob*) said to Far-oh,

> "The days of the years of my sojourning are a hundred and thirty years. Few וְרָעִים (and evil ones) have been the days of the years of my life, and they have not reached אֶת the days of the years of the lives of my ancestors in the days of their sojourning."

(10) And Ya-a-kov (*Jacob*) blessed אֶת Far-oh, and he went out from the presence of Far-oh.

(11) And Yo-sef settled אֶת his father וְאֶת (*and *) his brothers, and he gave them property in the land of Mitz-ra-yim (*Egypt*) in the best part of the land, in the land of Ra-m'ses, as Far-oh had instructed.

(12) And Yo-sef provided אֶת his father וְאֶת (*and *) his brothers וְאֵת (*and *) all the household of his father with food, according to the number of their children.

Genesis ~ 47

Joseph Buys The Livestock

(13) Now there was no food in all the land, for the famine was very severe. And the land of Mitz-ra-yim (*Egypt*) fainted, with the land of K'na-an, on account of the famine.

(14) And Yo-sef collected אֶת all the money found in the land of Mitz-ra-yim (*Egypt*) and in the land of K'na-an in exchange for the grain that they were buying. And Yo-sef brought אֶת the money into the house of Far-oh.

(15) And when the money was spent in the land of Mitz-ra-yim (*Egypt*) and from the land of K'na-an, all of Mitz-ra-yim (*Egypt*) came to Yo-sef, saying,

> *"Give us food! Why should we die before you? For the money is used up."*

(16) And Yo-sef said,

> *"Give your livestock and I will give you food in exchange for your livestock if your money is used up."*

(17) So they brought אֶת their herds to Yo-sef, and Yo-sef gave food to them in exchange for horses, their flocks, and their cattle and donkeys. And he provided them with food in exchange for all their livestock that year.

Joseph Buys The Land

(18) When that year ended, they came to him in the following year and said to him,

> *"We cannot hide* מֵאֲדֹנִי *(from my lord) that our money and livestock belong to* אֲדֹנִי *(my lord). Nothing remains before* אֲדֹנִי *(my lord) except our bodies and our land."*

Level One   בְּרֵאשִׁית ~ מז

(19)

> "Why should we die in front of you, both we and our land? Buy אֹתָנוּ (* us) וְאֶת (and *) our ground in exchange for food, then we and our land will be servants to Far-oh. Then give us seed and we shall live and not die, and the land will not become desolate."

(20) And Yo-sef bought אֶת all the ground of Mitz-ra-yim (*Egypt*) for Far-oh, for Mitz-ra-yim (*Egypt*) sold each man his field, for the famine was severe upon them. And the land became for Far-oh.

(21) וְאֶת (and *) the people, he transferred אֹתוֹ (* him) to the cities, from one end of the territory of Mitz-ra-yim (*Egypt*) to the other.

(22) Only the land of the priests he did not buy, for there was an allotment for the priests מֵאֵת (*from *) Far-oh, and they ate on אֶת the allotment that Far-oh gave to them. Therefore, they did not sell אֶת their ground.

(23) And Yo-sef said to the people,

> "Look, I have bought אֶתְכֶם (* you) today וְאֶת (and *) your ground for Far-oh. Here is seed for you so you can sow אֶת the ground."

(24)

> "And it shall happen that at the harvest, you must give a fifth to Far-oh and four-fifths shall be yours, as seed for the field and for your food and for those who are in your households, and as food for your little ones."

(25) And they said,

> "You have saved our lives. If we have found favor in the eyes of אֲדֹנִי (*my lord*), we will be servants to Far-oh."

(26) So Yo-sef made אֹתָהּ (* *it*) for a statute unto this day concerning the land of Mitz-ra-yim (*Egypt*): one fifth to Far-oh. Only the land of the priests alone did not belong to Far-oh.

Israel's Final Request

(27) So Yis-ra-el settled in the land of Mitz-ra-yim (*Egypt*), in the land of Go-shen. And they acquired possessions in it and were fruitful and multiplied greatly.

(28) And Ya-a-kov (*Jacob*) lived in the land of Mitz-ra-yim (*Egypt*) seventeen years. And the days of Ya-a-kov (*Jacob*), the years of his life, were a hundred and forty-seven years.

(29) When the time of Yis-ra-el's death drew near, he called to his son, to Yo-sef. And he said to him,

> *"If I have found favor in your eyes, please put your hand under my thigh, that you might vow to deal kindly and faithfully with me. Please do not bury me in Mitz-ra-yim (Egypt)."*

(30)

> *"But let me lie with my ancestors. Carry me out of Mitz-ra-yim (Egypt) and bury me in their burial site."*

And he said,

> *"I will do according to your word."*

(31) Then he said,

> *"Swear to me."*

And he swore to him. Then Yis-ra-el bowed himself on the head of the bed.

Chapter 48

Israel Adopts Ephraim And Manasseh

(1) And it happened that after these things, it was said to Yo-sef,

"Behold, your father is ill."

And he took אֶת two of his sons with him אֶת M'na-sheh וְאֶת (and *) Ef-ra-yim.

(2) And it was told to Ya-a-kov (*Jacob*),

"Behold, your son Yo-sef has come to you."

Then Yis-ra-el strengthened himself and he sat up in the bed.

(3) Then Ya-a-kov (*Jacob*) said to Yo-sef

אֵל שַׁדַּי נִרְאָה (*El Almighty appeared*) to me in Luz, in the land of K'na-an וַיְבָרֶךְ אֹתִי (*and He blessed * me*).

(4)

וַיֹּאמֶר (*And He said*) to me,

הִנְנִי מַפְרְךָ

וְהִרְבִּיתִךָ

וּנְתַתִּיךָ לִקְהַל עַמִּים

Behold, I will make you fruitful
and make you increase,
and I give you for an assembly of peoples.

Genesis ~ 48

וְנָתַתִּי אֶת-הָאָרֶץ הַזֹּאת

לְזַרְעֲךָ אַחֲרֶיךָ

אֲחֻזַּת עוֹלָם

And I will give * this land
to your seed after you
as an everlasting possession.

(5)

"And now, your two sons who were born to you in the land of Mitz-ra-yim (Egypt) before my coming to you in Mitz-ra-yim (Egypt), are mine. Ef-ra-yim and M'na-sheh shall be as R'u-ven and Shim-on are to me."

(6)

"And your children whom you father after them shall be yours. By the name of their brothers they shall be called, with respect to their inheritance."

(7)

"As for me, when I came to Pad-de-nah~A-ram, Ra-khel died to my sorrow in the land of K'na-an on the way when there was still some distance to go to Ef-ra-tah. And I buried her there on the way to Ef-ra-tah, that is Bet~Le-khem."

Israel Blesses Ephraim And Manasseh

(8) When Yis-ra-el saw אֵת the sons of Yo-sef he said,

"Who are these?"

Level One   בְּרֵאשִׁית ~ מח

(9) Then Yo-sef said to his father,

"They are my sons whom נָתַן אֱלֹהִים (Elohim gave) to me in this."

And he said,

"Please bring them to me that I may bless them."

(10) Now the eyes of Yis-ra-el were dim on account of old age; he was not able to see. So he brought אֹתָם (* them) near to him, and he kissed them and embraced them.

(11) And Yis-ra-el said to Yo-sef,

"I did not expect to see your face and behold אֱלֹהִים (Elohim) has also let אֹתִי (* me) see אֵת your seed."

(12) Then Yo-sef removed אֹתָם (* them) from his knees and bowed down with his face to the ground.

(13) And Yo-sef took אֵת the two of them אֵת Ef-ra-yim at his right to the left of Yis-ra-el וְאֵת (and *) M'na-sheh at his left to the right of Yis-ra-el. And he brought them near to him.

(14) And Yis-ra-el stretched out אֵת his right hand and put it on the head of Ef-ra-yim, now he was the younger וְאֵת (and *) his left hand on the head of M'na-sheh, crossing אֵת his hands, for M'na-sheh was the firstborn.

(15) And he blessed אֵת Yo-sef and said,

הָאֱלֹהִים (the Elohim) before Whom my fathers, Av-ra-ham and Yitz-khak (Isaac), walked, הָאֱלֹהִים הָרֹעֶה אֹתִי (the Elohim, the One shepherding * me) all my life unto this day."

Genesis ~ 48

(16)

הַמַּלְאָךְ הַגֹּאֵל אֹתִי *(The Messenger, the One redeeming * me) from all* רָע *(evil)* יְבָרֵךְ *(He shall bless)* אֶת *the young men. And through them let my name be perpetuated, and the name of my fathers, Av-ra-ham and Yitz-khak (Isaac). And let them multiply into many in the midst of the land."*

(17) When Yo-sef saw that his father put his right hand on the head of Ef-ra-yim, he was displeased. And he took hold of his father's hand to remove אֹתָהּ *(* it)* from the head of Ef-ra-yim over to the head of M'na-sheh.

(18) And Yo-sef said to his father,

"Not so, my father; because this one is the firstborn. Put your right hand upon his head."

(19) But his father refused and said,

"I know, my son; I know. He also shall become a people, and he also shall be great, but his younger brother shall be greater than him, and his seed shall become a multitude of nations."

(20) So he blessed them that day, saying,

"In you He shall bless Yis-ra-el, saying,

יְשִׂמְךָ אֱלֹהִים כְּאֶפְרַיִם וְכִמְנַשֶּׁה *(Elohim shall place you like Ef-ra-yim and like M'na-sheh).' "*

So he placed אֶת Ef-ra-yim before M'na-sheh.

(21) And Yis-ra-el said to Yo-sef,

| Level One | בְּרֵאשִׁית ~ מח |

"Behold, I am about to die וְהָיָה אֱלֹהִים (and Elohim will be) with you וְהֵשִׁיב אֶתְכֶם (and He will restore * you) to the land of your fathers."

(22)

"And I give to you Sh'khem rather than your brothers, which I took from the hand of the E-mo-ri (Amorite) by my sword and with my bow."

Chapter 49

Israel's Final Words

(1) Then Ya-a-kov (Jacob) called his sons and said,

> "Gather together so that I can tell you אֵת what will happen to אֶתְכֶם (* you) in days to come."

(2)

> "Assemble and hear, O sons of Ya-a-kov (Jacob). Listen to Yis-ra-el your father."

----

(3)

> "**R'u-ven**, אַתָּה (you) are my firstborn, my strength, and the firstfruit of my vigor, excelling in rank and excelling in power."

(4)

> "Unstable as water, you shall not excel any longer, for you went upon the bed of your father, then defiled it. You went upon my couch!"

----

(5)

> "**Shim-on and Le-vi** are brothers; weapons of violence are their broadswords."

Level One   בְּרֵאשִׁית ~ מט

(6)
"Let my soul not come into their council. Let not my glory be united in their assembly. For in their anger they killed a man, and at their pleasure they hamstrung a bull."

(7)
"Cursed be their anger, for it is fierce, and their wrath, for it is cruel. I will divide them in Ya-a-kov (Jacob), and I will scatter them in Yis-ra-el."

----

(8)
"Y'hu-dah, your brothers shall praise אַתָּה (you). Your hand shall be on the neck of your enemies. The sons of your father shall bow down to you."

(9)
"Y'hu-dah is a lion's cub. From the prey, my son, you have gone up. He bowed down; he crouched like a lion and as a lioness. Who shall rouse him?"

(10)
"The scepter shall not depart from Y'hu-dah, nor the ruler's staff between his feet, until tranquility comes. And to him shall be the obedience of nations."

(11)
"Binding his donkey to the vine and his donkey's colt to the choice vine, he washes his clothing in the wine and his garment in the blood of grapes."

(12)

"Flushed eyes from wine, and white teeth from milk."

----

(13)

"**Z'vu-lun** shall settle by the shore of the sea. He shall become a haven for ships, and his border shall be at Sidon."

----

(14)

"**Yis-sas-khar** is a strong donkey, crouching between the sheepfolds."

(15)

"He saw a resting place that was טוֹב (good) וְאֶת (and *) the land that was pleasant. So he bowed his shoulder to the burden and became a servant of forced labor."

----

(16)

"**Dan** shall judge his people as one of the tribes of Yis-ra-el."

(17)

"Dan shall be a serpent on the way, a viper on the road that bites the heels of a horse, so that its rider falls backward."

(18)

"I wait for Your salvation יהוה (YHVH)

Level One   בְּרֵאשִׁית ~ מט

---

(19)

"Bandits shall attack **Gad**, but he shall attack their heels."

---

(20)

"**A-sher**'s food is delicious, and he shall provide from the king's delicacies."

---

(21)

"**Naf-ta-li** is a doe running free that puts forth beautiful words."

---

(22)

"**Yo-sef** is the bough of a fruitful vine, a fruitful bough by a spring. His daughters climb over the wall."

(23)

"The archers fiercely attacked him. They shot arrows at him and were hostile to him."

(24)

"But his bow remained in a steady position; his arms were made agile by the hands of אֲבִיר יַעֲקֹב (the Mighty One of Ya-a-kov/Jacob), from there is רֹעֶה (a Shepherd) אֶבֶן יִשְׂרָאֵל (the Rock of Yis-ra-el)."

(25)

מֵאֵל אָבִיךָ *(From the El of your father)* וְיַעְזְרֶךָּ *(And He will help you)* וְאֵת שַׁדַּי *(and * the Almighty)* וִיבָרְכֶךָּ *(and He will bless you)* with the blessings of the sky above, blessings of the deep that crouches beneath, blessings of the breasts and the womb."

(26)

"The blessings of your father are superior to the blessings of my ancestors, to the bounty of the everlasting hills. May they be on the head of Yo-sef, and on the forehead of the prince of his brothers."

----

(27)

"**Ben-ya-min** is a devouring wolf, devouring the prey in the morning, and dividing the plunder in the evening."

Death Of Jacob

(28) All these are the twelve tribes of Yis-ra-el, and this is what their father said to them when he blessed אוֹתָם *(* them)*, each man according to their blessing, he blessed אֹתָם *(* them)*.

(29) Then he instructed אוֹתָם *(* them)* and said to them,

"I am about to be gathered to my people. Bury אֹתִי *(* me)* among my fathers in the cave that is in the field of Ef-ron the Khit-ti (Hittite)."

(30)

"In the cave that is in the field of Makh-pe-lah that is before Mam-re in the land of K'na-an, which Av-ra-ham bought with אֶת the field

Level One   בְּרֵאשִׁית ~ מט

(31)

מֵאֵת *(from *) Ef-ron the Khit-ti (Hittite) as a burial site."*

"There they buried אֵת Av-ra-ham וְאֵת *(and *)* Sa-rah his wife. There they buried אֵת Yitz-khak (Isaac) וְאֵת *(and *)* Riv-kah (Rebekah) his wife. And there I buried אֵת Le-ah."

(32)

"The field and the cave which are in it were purchased מֵאֵת *(from *) the sons of Khet."*

(33) When Ya-a-kov (Jacob) finished instructing אֵת his sons he drew his feet up to the bed. Then he took his last breath and was gathered to his people.

Chapter 50

Jacob's Funeral

(1) Then Yo-sef fell on the face of his father and wept upon him and kissed him.

(2) And Yo-sef instructed אֶת his servants אֶת the physicians to embalm אֶת his father. So the physicians embalmed אֶת Yis-ra-el.

(3) Forty days were required for it, for thus are the days required for embalming. And Mitz-ra-yim (*Egypt*) wept for אֹתוֹ (*him*) seventy days.

(4) When the days of his weeping had passed, Yo-sef spoke to the household of Far-oh, saying,

> "If I have found favor in your eyes, please speak in the hearing of Far-oh, saying,"

(5)

> 'My father made me swear, saying,
>
>> "Behold, I am about to die. In the tomb that I have hewed out for myself in the land of K'na-an, there you must bury me."
>
> 'So then, please let me go up and let me bury אֶת my father; and I will return.' "

(6) Then Far-oh said,

> "Go up and bury אֶת your father as he made you swear."

(7) So Yo-sef went up to bury אֶת his father. And all the servants of Far-oh, the

Level One   בְּרֵאשִׁית ~ נ

elders of his household, and all the elders of the land of Mitz-ra-yim (*Egypt*), went up with אֹתוֹ (* *him*),

(8) with all the household of Yo-sef, his brothers, and the household of his father. They left only their little children and their flocks and their herds in the land of Go-shen.

(9) And there also went up with him chariots and horsemen. The company was very great.

(10) When they came to Go-ren~Ha-a-tad, the threshing floor of Atad,, which was beyond the Yar-den (*Jordan*), they lamented there with a very great and sorrowful wailing. And he made a mourning ceremony for his father seven days.

(11) And when the K'na-a-ni (*Canaanite*), the inhabitants of the land, saw אֶת- הָאֵבֶל (* *the mourning*) at Go-ren~Ha-a-tad, the threshing floor of Atad, they said,

"This is a severe אֵבֶל (*mourning*) for Mitz-ra-yim (*Egypt*)."

Therefore, its name was called אָבֵל מִצְרַיִם (Abel-Mizraim), which is beyond the Yar-den (*Jordan*).

(12) Thus his sons did to him just as he had instructed them.

(13) And his sons carried אֹתוֹ (* *him*) to the land of K'na-an and buried אֹתוֹ (* *him*) in the cave of the field of Makh-pe-lah, where Av-ra-ham bought אֶת the field as a burial site מֵאֵת (*from* *) Ef-ron the Khit-ti (*Hittite*) before Mam-re.

Joseph's Brothers Repent

(14) And after burying אֶת his father, Yo-sef returned to Mitz-ra-yim (*Egypt*), he and his brothers and all who had gone up with אֹתוֹ (* *him*) to bury אֶת his father.

(15) And when the brothers of Yo-sef saw that their father was dead, they said,

"It may be that Yo-sef will hold a grudge against us and pay us back dearly for אֵת all הָרָעָה (the evil) that we did to אֹתוֹ (* him)."

(16) So they sent word to Yo-sef saying,

"Your father commanded us before his death, saying,"

(17)

'Thus you must say to Yo-sef,

"O, please now forgive the transgression of your brothers and their sin, for they did רָעָה (evil) to you." So now, please forgive the transgression of the servants of אֱלֹהֵי אָבִיךָ (the Elohim of your father)."

And Yo-sef wept when they spoke to him.

(18) Then his brothers went also and fell before him and said,

"Behold, we are your servants."

(19) Then Yo-sef said to them,

"Do not be afraid, for am I in the place of אֱלֹהִים (Elohim)."

(20)

"As for you, you planned רָעָה (evil) against me, but אֱלֹהִים חֲשָׁבָהּ (Elohim planned it) לְטֹבָה (for good), in order to do this, to keep many people alive as it is today."

(21)

"So then, do not be afraid. I myself will sustain אֶתְכֶם (* you) וְאֵת (and *) your little ones."

282

Level One

בְּרֵאשִׁית ~ נ

And he consoled אוֹתָם (* them) and spoke kindly to them.

Death Of Joseph

(22) So Yo-sef remained in Mitz-ra-yim (*Egypt*), he and the house of his father. And Yo-sef lived one hundred and ten years.

(23) And Yo-sef saw the sons of Ef-ra-yim to the third generation. Moreover, the children of Ma-khir, son of M'na-sheh, were born on the knees of Yo-sef.

(24) And Yo-sef said to his brothers,

> "*I am about to die* וֵאלֹהִים פָּקֹד יִפְקֹד אֶתְכֶם *(and Elohim will certainly visit * you)* וְהֶעֱלָה אֶתְכֶם *(and He will bring up * you) from this land to the land that* נִשְׁבַּע לְאַבְרָהָם לְיִצְחָק וּלְיַעֲקֹב *(he swore to Abraham, to Isaac, and to Jacob)."*

(25) And Yo-sef made אֶת the sons of Yis-ra-el swear an oath, saying,

> פָּקֹד יִפְקֹד אֱלֹהִים אֶתְכֶם *(Elohim will surely visit * you), and you shall bring up* אֶת *my bones from here."*

(26) So Yo-sef died, being one hundred and ten years old. They embalmed אֹתוֹ (* him) and he was placed in a coffin in Mitz-ra-yim (*Egypt*).

Index

Not all the words that have been restored in
The Progressive Torah: Genesis
are represented in this index, only the Hebrew that appears in the blue
font in the color-coded edition.

English	Pronunciation	Hebrew
in the head of	/b're - shit/	בְּרֵאשִׁית
in the summit of	ית - רֵאשׁ - בְּ	
	of - head / top / leader - in/ on	

Please note that the English translation is not the full picture of the word or a complete translation of the word, but it is rather a simplified translation.

Level One   בְּרֵאשִׁית

English	Pronunciation	Hebrew
Mighty One	/a - vir/	אֲבִיר
a stone	/e - ven/	אֶבֶן
lord/master	/a - don/	אָדוֹן
my lord/master	/a - do - nai/	אֲדֹנָי
lord/master of me	/a - do - nai/	אֲדֹנַי
	/a - do - ni/	אֲדֹנִי
		אֲדֹנָ - ִי
		אֲדֹנַ - ִי
		אֲדֹנ - ִי
		lord of - me
lord/master of	/a - do - nay/	אֲדֹנֵי
		אֲדֹנֵ - ִי
		lord - of
their lord/master	/a - do - nay - hem/	אֲדֹנֵיהֶם
lord/master of them		אֲדֹנֵ - ִי - הֶם
(them = masculine)		lord - of - them
his lord/master	/a - do - nav/	אֲדֹנָיו
lord/master of him		אֲדֹנָ - ִי - ו
		lord - of - him
your lord/master	/a - do - ney - kha/	אֲדֹנֶיךָ
lord/master of you		אֲדֹנֶ - ִי - ךָ
(you = masculine, single)		lord - of - you

285

Genesis ~ Index

Alef-Tav you	/ot - kha/		אוֹתְךָ
* you		ךָ -	אוֹת
(you = masculine, single)		you -	Alef Tav
Alef-Tav you	/o - takh/		אוֹתָךְ
* you		ךְ -	אוֹתָ
(you = feminine, single)		you -	Alef Tav
Alef-Tav them	/o - tam/		אוֹתָם
* them		ם -	אוֹתָ
(them = masculine)		them -	Alef Tav
God - Mighty One	/el/		אֵל
Everlasting God	/el o'lam/		אֵל עוֹלָם
God of eternity		עוֹלָם	אֵל -
God of uiverse		everlasting -	El
God Most High	/el el - yon/		אֵל עֶלְיוֹן
		עֶלְיוֹן	אֵל -
		Most High -	El
God seeing me	/el ro - i/		אֵל רָאִי
		רָא -	אֵל -
		me - seeing -	El
God Almighty	/el sha - dai/		אֵל שַׁדַּי
		שַׁדַּי	אֵל -
		Almighty -	El

286

Level One   בְּרֵאשִׁית

my God/gods	/e - lo - hai/		אֱלֹהַי
gods/God of me	/e - lo - hai/		אֱלֹהָי
		ִ	אֱלֹה -
		ָ	אֱלֹה -
		of me -	elohim
God/gods of...	/e - lo - hay/		אֱלֹהֵי
		ֵ	אֱלֹה -
		of -	elohim
your God/gods	/e - lo - hey - khah/		אֱלֹהֶיךָ
God/gods of you		ךָ - ֶי	אֱלֹה -
(you = masculine, single)		you - of -	elohim
your God/gods	/e - lo - hay - khem/		אֱלֹהֵיכֶם
God/gods of you		כֶם - ֵי	אֱלֹה -
(you = masculine, plural)		you - of -	elohim
God/gods	/e - lo - him/		אֱלֹהִים
		ִים	אֱלֹה -
		(plural ending) -	elohim
Alef-Tav *	/et/ or /et/		אֵת

* *The Alef-Tav is a complex matter. Some say it is merely a direct object marker. Others say it is a much more complex issue than that. For this reason it is not easily translated by one or two words, therefore, it is represented in the text of the Progressive Torah by an " * ".*

287

Genesis ~ Index

you	/at/		אַתְּ
(you = feminine, singular)	/at/		אָתְּ
Alef-Tav her/it	/o - tah/		אֹתָהּ
* her/it	/i - tah/		אִתָהּ
		ה -	אֹת
		ה -	אִתְ
		her -	Alef Tav
you	/a - tah/		אַתָּה
(you = masculine, single)	/a - tah/		אָתָּה
Alef-Tav them	/et - hem/		אֶתְהֶם
* them		הֶם -	אֶתְ
(them = masculine)		them -	Alef Tav
Alef-Tav them	/et - hen/		אֶתְהֶן
* them		הֶן -	אֶתְ
(them = feminine)		them -	Alef Tav
Alef-Tav him/it	/o - to/		אֹתוֹ
* him/it	/i - to/		אִתּוֹ
		וֹ -	אֹת
		וֹ -	אִתְ
		him -	Alef Tav

288

Level One   בְּרֵאשִׁית

Alef-Tav me * me 	/o - ti/		אֹתִי
	/i - ti/		אִתִי
		־ י	אֹת
		־ י	אִת
		me	Alef Tav -
Alef-Tav you * you (you = masculine, single)	/ot - kha/		אֹתְךָ
	/it - kha/		אִתְךָ
		־ ךָ	אֹת
		־ ךָ	אִת
		you	Alef Tav -
Alef-Tav you * you (you = feminine, single)	/o - takh/		אֹתָךְ
	/i - takh/		אִתָךְ
		־ ךְ	אֹת
		־ ךְ	אִת
		you	Alef Tav -
Alef-Tav you * you (you = masculine, plural)	/it - khem/		אִתְכֶם
	/et - khem/		אֶתְכֶם
		כֶם	אִת
		כֶם	אֶת
		you	Alef Tav -

Alef-Tav them * them (them = masculine)	/o - tam/	אֹתָם
	/i - tam/	אִתָּם
	ם - אֹת	
	ם - אִתָּ	
	them - Alef Tav	
Alef-Tav us * us	/o - ta - nu/	אֹתָנוּ
	/i - ta - nu/	אִתָּנוּ
	נוּ - אֹת	
	נוּ - אִתָּ	
	us - Alef Tav	
you (you = masculine, plural)	/a - tem/	אַתֶּם
in/on the God/gods	/ve - lo - him/	בֵּאלֹהִים
	ים - אלֹה - בֵּ	
	(plural ending) - elohim - in/on	
in the good	/ba - tov/	בַּטּוֹב
	טוֹב - בַּ	
	good - in/on the	
in/on YHVH	/ba -YHVH/	בַּיהוָה
	יהוה - בַּ	
	YHVH - in/on	

Level One   בְּרֵאשִׁית

Beth-El the house of God	/b<u>e</u>t - <u>e</u>l/	בֵּית-אֵל
		בֵּית - אֵל
		house of - El
in peace/ completeness	/b'sha - lom/	בְּשָׁלוֹם
		בְּ - שָׁלוֹם
		in/on - peace
the God or the God of...	/ha - <u>e</u>l/	הָאֵל
		הָ - אֵל
		the - El
the God/gods	/ha - e - lo - him/	הָאֱלֹהִים
		הָ - אֱלֹה - ִים
		the - elohim - (plural ending)
the good	/ha - tov/	הַטוֹב
		הַ - טוֹב
		the - good
the good ones (*feminine*)	/ha - to - vot/	הַטוֹבוֹת
		הַ - טוֹב - וֹת
		the - good - (plural ending)
the good ones (*feminine*)	/ha - to - vot/	הַטֹבֹת
		הַ - טוֹב - ת
		the - good - (plural ending)

the messenger	/ha - mal - akh/	הַמַּלְאָךְ
		הַ - מַלְאָךְ
		the - messenger
the messengers	/ha - mal - a - khim/	הַמַּלְאָכִים
		הַ - מַלְאָכ - ים
		the - messenger - (plural ending)
the evil	/ha - ra - ah/	הָרָעָה
		הָ - רָע - ה
		the - evil - (feminine ending)
the one shepherding / the shepherd	/ha - ro - eh/	הָרֹעֶה
		הָ - רֹעֶה
		the - shepherd
the peace/ completeness	/ha - sha - lom/	הַשָּׁלוֹם
		הַ - שָׁלוֹם
		the - peace
the Judge of	/ha - sho - fet/	הַשֹּׁפֵט
		הַ - שֹׁפֵט
		the - judge
and my lord/master / and lord/master of me	/va - do - ni/	וַאדֹנִי
		וַ - אדֹנ - י
		and - lord - me

Level One   בְּרֵאשִׁית

and God	/v'el/	וְאֵל
		וְ - אֵל
		and - El
and the God/gods of	/ve - lo - hay/	וֵאלֹהֵי
		וֵ - אלֹה - ֵי
		and - elohim - of
and God/gods	/ve - lo - him/	וֵאלֹהִים
		וֵ - אלֹה - ִים
		and - elohim - (plural ending)
and *Alef-Tav*	/v'et/	וְאֵת
and *		וְ - אֵת
		and - Alef Tav
and you	/v'a - tah/	וְאַתָּה
(you = masculine, single)	/va - a - tah/	וְאָתָּה
		וְ - אַתָּה
		וָ - אָתָּה
		and - you
and *Alef Tav* him/it	/v'ot - o/	וְאֹתוֹ
and * him/it		וְ - אֹת - וֹ
		and - Alef Tav - him
and *Alef-Tav* you	/v'o - takh/	וְאֹתָךְ
and * you		וְ - אֹתָ - ךְ
(you = feminine, single)		and - Alef Tav - you

Genesis ~ Index

and the God/gods	/v'ha - e - lo - him/		וְהָאֱלֹהִים
		וְ - הָ - אֱלֹה - ים	
		and - the - elohim - (plural ending)	
and the evil ones (feminine)	/v'ha - ra - ot/		וְהָרָעוֹת
		וְ - הָ - רָע - וֹת	
		and - the - evil - (plural ending)	
and YHVH	/va - YHVH/		וַיהוה
		וַ - יהוה	
		and - YHVH	
and good	/v'tov/		וְטוֹב
		וְ - טוֹב	
		and - good	
and good ones (feminine)	/v'to - vot/		וְטֹבוֹת
		וְ - טוֹב - וֹת	
		and - good - (plural ending)	
and to/for a lord/master	/ul - a - don/		וּלְאָדוֹן
		וּ - לְ - אָדוֹן	
		and - to/for - lord	
and the Spirit of God / and the wind of God / and the breath of God	/ru - akh e - lo - him/		וְרוּחַ אֱלֹהִים
		וְ - רוּחַ - אֱלֹה - ים	
		and - spirit of - elohim - (plural ending)	

Level One   בְּרֵאשִׁית

an interval *(space to freely breath)*	/v're - vakh/	וְרֶוַח
		וְ - רֶוַח
		and - interval
and evil	/va - ra/	וָרָע
		וָ - רָע
		and - evil
and evil ones *(feminine)* *(masculine)*	/v'ra - ot/	וְרָעוֹת
	/v'ra - im/	וְרָעִים
	וְ - רָע - וֹת	
	וְ - רָע - ים	
	and - evil - (plural ending)	
YHVH the name of our Creator, *El of Abraham, Isaac, and Jacob*	various pronunciations… various reasons…	יהוה
he will see [*to it*] he will provide	/yir - eh/	יִרְאֶה
		יִ - רְאֶה
		he - will see
like/as God/gods	/ke - lo - him/	כֵּאלֹהִים
	כֵּ - אלֹה - ים	
	like/as - elohim - (plural ending)	

like/as the good	/ka - tov/	כָּטוֹב
		כַּ - טוֹב
		like/as the - good
good ones (masculine)	/to - vim/	טוֹבִים
		טוֹב - ים
		good - (plural ending)
good of	/to - vat/	טֹבַת
good ones (feminine)	/to - vot/	טֹבֹת
		טֹב - ת
		good - (plural ending)
good / good of	/tov/	טוֹב
good / good of	/to - vah/	טוֹבָה
		טוֹב - ָה
		good - (feminine ending)
to/for a lord/master	/l'a - don/	לְאָדוֹן
		לְ - אָדוֹן
		to/for - lord
to/for my lord/master to for lord/master of me	/la - do - ni/ /la - do - nai/	לַאדֹנִי לַאדֹנָי
		לְ - אֲדֹן - ִי
		לְ - אֲדֹן - ָי
		to/for - lord - me

Level One   בְּרֵאשִׁית

to/for their lord/master to/for lord/master of them *(them = masculine)*	/la - a - do - nay - hem/	לַאֲדֹנֵיהֶם
	לְ - אֲדֹן - יֵ - הֶם	
	to/for - lord - of - them	
to/for God	/la - el/	לָאֵל
	/l'el/	לְאֵל
		לְ - אֵל
		לְ - אֵל
	to/for - El	
to/for God/gods of	/le - lo - hay/	לֵאלֹהֵי
	לְ - אלה - ֵי	
	to/for - elohim - of	
to/for God/the gods	/le - lo - him/	לֵאלֹהִים
	לְ - אלה - ִים	
	to/for - elohim - *(plural ending)*	
to/for good	/l'to-vah/	לְטֹבָה
	לְ - טֹב - ה	
	to/for - good - *(feminine ending)*	
to/for YHVH	/la - YHVH/	לַיהוה
	לַ - יהוה	
	to/for - YHVH	

Genesis ~ Index

to/for wind to/for the breath to/for the spirit	/l'ru - akh/		לָרוּחַ
		רוּחַ - לְ	
		spirit - to/for	
to/for evil	/la - ro - a/		לָרֹעַ
	/l'ra - ah/		לְרָעָה
		רֹעַ - לְ	
		הָ - רָע - לְ	
		(feminine ending) - evil - to/for	
to/for peace completeness	/l'sha - lom/		לְשָׁלוֹם
		שָׁלוֹם - לְ	
		peace - to/for	
from my lord/master from lord/master of me	/may - a - do - ni/		מֵאֲדֹנִי
		ִי - אֲדֹן - מֵ	
		me - lord - from	
from God	/me - el/		מֵאֵל
		אֵל - מֵ	
		El - from	
from *Alef-Tav* from *	/me - et/		מֵאֵת
		אֵת - מֵ	
		Alef Tav - from	

Level One   בְּרֵאשִׁית

from *Alef-Tav* him/it	/me - o - to/	מֵאִתּוֹ
from * him/it	מֵ - אֵת - וֹ	
	from - Alef Tav - him	
from *Alef-Tav* me	/me - i - ti/	מֵאִתִּי
from * me	מֵ - אֵת - י	
	from - Alef Tav - me	
from *Alef-Tav* you	/me - it - khem/	מֵאִתְּכֶם
from * you	מֵ - אֵת - כֶם	
(you = masculine, plural)	from - Alef Tav - you	
from *Alef Tav* them	/me - i - tam/	מֵאִתָּם
from * them	מֵ - אֵת - ם	
(them = masculine)	from - Alef Tav - them	
from YHVH	/me - YHVH/	מֵיהוה
	מֵ - יהוה	
	from - YHVH	
from the good	/mi - tuv/	מִטּוּב
	מִ - טוּב	
	from - good	
messenger	/mal - akh/	מַלְאָךְ
his messenger	/mal - a - kho/	מַלְאָכוֹ
messenger of him	מַלְאָכ - וֹ	
	messenger - of him	

messengers of	/mal - a - khay/		מַלְאֲכֵי
		ִי -	מַלְאָכ
	(*plural ending*) of	-	messenger
messengers	/mal - a - khim/		מַלְאָכִים
	ִים -		מַלְאָכ
	(*plural ending*)	-	messenger
from the Tree of Life	/me - etz ha - khai - yim/		מֵעֵץ הַחַיִּים
	מֵ - עֵץ	ה -	חַיִּים
	from - tree	- the	- lives
the Most High	/el - yon/		עֶלְיוֹן
the Tree of Life	/etz ha - khai - yim/		עֵץ הַחַיִּים
	עֵץ	ה -	חַיִּים
	tree	the -	lives
creator/owner of	/ko - ne/		קֹנֵה
spirit/wind/breath	/ru - akh/		רוּחַ
the Spirit of God	/ru - akh e - lo - him/		רוּחַ אֱלֹהִים
the wind of God	רוּחַ - אֱלֹה - ִים		
the breath of God	spirit of - elohim - (*plural ending*)		
his spirit/breath/wind	/ru - kho/		רוּחוֹ
spirit of him	רוּחַ - וֹ		
	spirit of - him		

Level One   בְּרֵאשִׁית

my spirit/breath/wind	/ru - khi/	רוּחִי
spirit of me		רוּח - ִ
		spirit of - me
evil	/ra/	רַע
evil ones (feminine)	/ra - ot/	רָעוֹת
		רַע - וֹת
		evil - (plural ending)
evil	/ra - ah/	רָעָה
		רָע - ָה
		evil - (feminine ending)
shepherd	/ro - eh/	רֹעֶה
shepherdess	/ro - ah/	רֹעָה
shepherds of	/ro - ay/	רֹעֵי
my shepherds	/ro - ai/	רֹעַי
shepherds of me		רֹע - ַ
		shepherd - of me
your shepherds	/ro - ey - kha/	רֹעֶיךָ
shepherds of you		רֹע - ֶי - ךָ
		shepherd - of - you
evil ones	/ra - im/	רָעִים
		רַע - ִים
		evil - (plural ending)
peace/completeness	/sha - lom/	שָׁלוֹם
He who suffices	/sha - dai/	שַׁדַּי

FINAL NOTES

We hope your journey has been enriched and you are blessed through the production of The Progressive Torah series! Minister 2 Others would like to hear from you. If you have comments or questions concerning our materials, or if you find errors in our projects, misspellings, or formatting issues. We work hard to provide quality materials, however, sometimes things can squeak by unnoticed. Your feedback is truly appreciated.

If you have enjoyed this production, please consider writing a review and letting others know about our materials.

Thanks!

                          Minister 2 Others
                          Minister2others.com

Like reading the stories found in the book of Genesis? Then you'll love our Ancient Texts and the Bible series! This ten volume set completely synchronizes the Bible, with the books of *Enoch, Jasher, and Jubilees;* making one harmonizing story out of the four!

Available in Easy Reader Edition and Expanded Edition!

www.ingramcontent.com/pod-product-compliance
Lightning Source LLC
Chambersburg PA
CBHW081333080526
44588CB00017B/2606